SHADOWING AND SURVEILLANCE

A COMPLETE GUIDEBOOK

by Burt Rapp

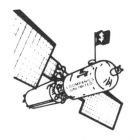

Loompanics Unlimited
Port Townsend, WA 98368

SHADOWING AND SURVEILLANCE
A Complete Guidebook
© 1986 by Loompanics Unlimited
All Rights Reserved
Printed in the USA

Published by:
Loompanics Unlimited
PO Box 1197
Port Townsend, WA 98368

ISBN: 0-915179-33-4
Library of Congress
  Card Catalog Number 85-082012

TABLE OF CONTENTS

INTRODUCTION

Surveillance and shadowing aren't techniques restricted to the police profession. Private citizens have need for them, too:

A man suspects his wife is cheating on him. He has to go to work daily, which gives her the opportunity. To confirm his suspicion, he places a microphone leading to a voice-operated tape recorder in the bedroom. Each evening, he checks the tape. Over several weeks, he finds that a male acquaintance of hers comes every Thursday, which is when the infidelity occurs. He doesn't know the name, or recognize the voice, so he arranges to take a Thursday off from work without telling his wife.

Borrowing the van of a friend who is unknown to his wife, he parks it down the street and stakes out his own house. He parks far enough away not to be conspicuous, and watches his street carefully. When he sees a car pull up in front of his house, he observes it through binoculars and writes down the license number, in case he should need this information later. He gets a good look at the man who enters his house, but doesn't recognize him. When the man leaves, three hours later, the husband follows his car, being careful not to be spotted, and in this way discovers where the guy lives.

We'll leave our hypothetical husband now. What he does with the information is his own business—our main interest is how he got it.

Let's examine another need:

A store owner becomes aware that one of his employees is ripping him off. He theorizes that this individual waits for him to leave the store on an errand, then slips out the back door with some merchandise to his car parked in the alley.

He decides on a plan. One day, telling the employees that he'll be gone for several hours, he leaves the store. He walks around the block to the mouth of the alley, and takes up a position where he can't be seen by passers-by on the street, but which permits him to watch the back door of his store and the employee's parking lot.

After an hour's wait he sees one of his employees come out carrying a box, which he puts in the trunk of his car. Going back to the store, he calls the employee into the office and confronts him.

We'll interrupt the story at this point, because the employer has several choices, and exploring them would take us beyond the scope of this chapter, although we'll get into theft later on in the book.

Let's take another example:

An employee suspects a fellow worker of being the company spy. It's just a suspicion, but he wants to check it out. He decides to tell his suspect a story that will reflect badly on another employee, and on which the boss will have to act. Later in the day, he hears through the company grapevine that there was a nasty confrontation between the boss and the subject of the story. Suspicion confirmed!

All of these incidents have something in common: The intelligent use of surveillance, shadowing, and counter-intelligence techniques without the need for elaborate, sophisticated, and expensive equipment. This book will deal with practical, everyday techniques of shadowing and surveillance, concentrating on methods within reach of the average reader.

Many such books concentrate on elaborate and expensive electronic equipment, which is plainly out of reach of anyone who has to live on a budget. This makes such books next to useless for most people. Instead, this book will concentrate on simple, practical, and easily applicable techniques. While there will be some discussion of exotic hardware, this will be to show that often the utility does not justify the expense, and the equipment is over-sold.

In the author's experience, many of the new gadgets, exotic or not, simply don't live up to expectations. They're almost never cost-effective, whatever the price, and most are priced out of the reach of the majority of people.

The emphasis will be on tactics rather than hardware. We'll explore both overt and covert surveillance, with only brief attention to the first, because it's not very complex or interesting. The emphasis will be on covert surveillance, because in some ways this is the more useful technique and the one most likely to produce dramatic results.

We'll explore physical surveillance, which is observation and shadowing, and electronic surveillance, "bugging," and note the techniques and tactics of each. We'll look at various technical aids, with the emphasis on simple and inexpensive means within the reach of Joe Citizen.

As Joe Citizen doesn't have the resources of an investigative agency behind him, and often can't even count on the help of a sympathetic friend, most of what follows will be geared toward the one-man operation. There will be some discussion of team tactics, because this book would be incomplete without it, and the lucky individual may be able to find an ally.

Most of the techniques and tactics that follow have had the aura of deep secrets shared only among the privileged few who staff our police and private investigative agencies. In fact, the techniques are simple enough for a high-school student to understand, and this leads to a suspicion that most of the secrecy has been to conceal how little these professionals really know.

While the techniques are basically simple, putting them into practice requires some dedication and skill. While surveillance is simple in concept, as is riding a bicycle, it's something that requires concentration and practice to learn.

FACT AND FICTION

Many of us pick up what we know about surveillance from the movies, television, and detective novels. Unfortunately, few of the novels and screenplays are written by policemen and professional investigators, and the scriptwriters who crank them out usually don't bother to check their facts. They're more concerned with dramatic impact, and attracting a large audience, and this shows in the conspicuous lack of accuracy in their work.

It's easy to note some of the more obvious errors, such as a reference to a safety on a revolver, or a silencer that fits on a revolver barrel and lets out only a "poof" when the gun discharges.

Less obvious are the errors in regard to techniques of surveillance and shadowing. We see the hero, often in a trench coat, following the suspect for a few yards, then a gunfight erupts and the story takes another direction. A fictional surveillance has the hero ducking into doorways and looking around furtively, but the real-life version is much more banal.

One of the few exceptions was the film *The French Connection.* "Popeye" Doyle, the narcotics detective, tailed his suspect through the streets of New York and into a subway station, finally losing him because the suspect "made" the tail. This sequence would make a good training film, because it showed moving surveillance as it really is.

We saw Popeye follow the suspect through the crowds in the streets of Manhattan, trying to keep him in sight yet staying far enough away so as not to be conspicuous. Popeye at one point broke his profile by taking off his hat and coat. As he was alone, and could not drop back to let a new face take over the close tail, the suspect finally made him and ditched him by boarding a subway train, entering just as the doors closed. Anyone seeing this sequence will realize the difficulties inherent in using a one-man tail with a subject who suspects that he might be followed and regularly takes precautions to discover the tail.

"Tails" sometimes fail, and this film showed one that did, and why and how it happened. That's realism.

In reality, a surveillance can be long, boring, and unproductive, while in the movies they're short and sweet. Anyone who embarks upon a stake-out must prepare himself to struggle to stay awake. A tail can take place in rain or snow, and can be very uncomfortable. There isn't much threat of physical danger, but at times a fistfight or shootout would be welcome to break up the tedium.

A film which showed some of the problems of a stake-out with realism is *Contract On Cherry Street*. Keeping a large warehouse under observation for many days is not as easy as it seems, even though the subject is large and stationary.

In reality, it's sometimes easier to tail a person for a thousand miles than for a thousand yards, if it involves an airplane trip. The shadower merely buys a ticket and boards the aircraft with the other passengers, secure in the knowledge that his subject will be within reach until they arrive at their destination. In the city streets, the task is much more demanding.

Another film which was very realistic was *Death Wish*, in which a middle-class man turned vigilante to avenge the death of his wife and the rape of his daughter. This film did not concentrate on non-stop action, but instead showed the practical difficulties faced by a man who has to go to work every day, and find the time to set himself up as a decoy during his off-hours. While the film had to compress the time scale, we nevertheless got the impression that he spent many hours walking through dangerous areas, waiting for a mugger to strike.

We often see the fictional hero as a master of disguise, changing his appearance radically to help him in his task. The Sherlock Holmes stories and films are good examples. In reality, disguise is very limited, and usually for the purpose of "breaking the profile" rather than radically changing appearance.

Another gimmick that has no place in real life is the mechanical license-plate bracket, as shown on James Bond's Aston-Martin, which flips up at the touch of a button to be replaced by one with a different number. If the subject sees an Aston-Martin sticking close to him in his rear-view mirror, he's not likely to be fooled by a change of license plate number. Such a car is as conspicuous on the street as a clown suit at a funeral.

With some of the fictional versions out of the way, let's turn to how it is in real life.

POLICE TECHNIQUES

OF SURVEILLANCE

The police have powers that ordinary citizens lack. First, they have their status as law enforcement officers, which is important because it gives them certain unofficial powers. In conducting interrogations of witnesses, for example, the police officer's badge enables him to get a degree of cooperation from citizens that, say, a journalist would not.

In the case of recalcitrant witnesses, the police have official powers that a private investigator would envy, although the police themselves constantly complain their powers are being eroded by capricious court decisions.

One such power is a search warrant, although today it's not as easy to obtain one as formerly. There must be an affidavit, supported by probable cause, which can be the result of direct observation, information from a "snitch," or other investigation. Serving a search warrant, however, brings the investigation out in the open, and is not a surreptitious activity.

The police also have access to public and private records, although it may be necessary to get a court order for some of them. Bank and hospital records, drivers license records and motor vehicle registrations are all open to them.

The police can also obtain a warrant to use a wiretap. Formerly, wiretaps were in more common use, as far as publicly disclosed information shows, but it's now a Federal crime to install a wiretap without a court order, and supposedly their use has declined, if we can believe the statistics that law enforcement agencies release infrequently.

What is clear is that it's necessary to have a court order to use wiretap information as evidence—otherwise, it's "tainted," and not admissible.

There's no way to know how many police wiretaps are in place, with or without a court order. The police can, by flashing a badge, get the cooperation of telephone company employees, apartment managers, and others who can help them install a wiretap or give them access to a place where they can.

Granted that a wiretap without a court order is illegal, but who's going to arrest the police? When they feel the need, they install a wiretap, secure in the knowledge that they're almost immune from prosecution.

Even without a court order, a wiretap is useful for developing information, or "leads." An intercepted conversation can provide the police with a fact that can open up a fruitful avenue in an investigation, and the resulting evidence can make it unnecessary to introduce the wiretapped conversation in court. Thus, many wiretaps can be useful even if it's clear from the start they will be inadmissible.

Another advantage the police have is an unequalled capacity to develop informants and informers. An "informant" is someone, not necessarily a criminal but perhaps a simple witness to a crime, who provides information to the police willingly, without coercion or reward. An "informer" is either in the pay of the police, or is a criminal working out a "deal" in which he supplies information in return for not being prosecuted.

With the paid informer, the police usually have a slush fund from which they get the money to buy information. This fund, a secret one budgeted under a title such as "contingency fund," is more than the private citizen can afford.

There's a problem with paid informers: bad information. As they're often criminals themselves, they have no qualms about concocting "information" they can sell. This is why criminal investigators feel uneasy with paid informers, because they've found through hard experience that what they're buying is often garbage.

They prefer to have a "twist" on their informers. A "twist" is a means of coercion. A criminal who is caught often has the choice of "cooperating" with the police or facing a trial and heavy sentence. "Cooperating" can get him a reduction of sentence, or even complete immunity. Much depends on when the criminal decides to cooperate. If he caves in before the police make out the arrest paperwork, he can work a deal in which he gets off completely. If he's already been arrested and arraigned, any deal depends heavily on how far the prosecutor is inclined to cooperate. He may agree to drop the charges, or to ask the judge for a reduced sentence. If he's a dedicated careerist, and running for re-election, he may want to prosecute to the fullest, whatever the potential value of the information the defendant might provide to the police.

This is often a point of contention between criminal investigators and public prosecutors. The investigator is usually quite willing to let a small offender go in order to get the big fish. The prosecutor, unless he's very intelligent and understanding, is typically set on prosecuting the people he has in hand, and is unlikely to accept the deferred gratification of a more important defendant at some time in the future. Usually, the prosecutor has no day-to-day control over a criminal investigation, and no influence on the outcome except by acceding to the wishes of the investigator who keeps all the cards in his hands. This isn't much incentive to cooperate, and is one source of organizational inefficiency.

The investigator, on the other hand, is likely to feel frustrated by an uncooperative prosecutor. Being a policeman, he's naturally suspicious, and reluctant to yield any control whatsoever to the prosecutor. It often goes so far that the investigator will withhold as much information as he can, fearful of "leaks." Experience has shown that the more people who are party to a confidential matter, the greater the chance of a leak.

There are other means of coercion available to the police, methods which would be illegal if a private citizen used them. It's worth a look at the meaning of legality, and its practical application, to understand this fully.

Offering money for information is bribery. A citizen who offers a bribe to a public official or to another citizen for an illegal purpose is committing a crime. If the police do it to a criminal, it's legal.

Obtaining compliance by threats is extortion. If the police threaten a criminal with prosecution unless he "cooperates," it doesn't create any waves.

Another means of gaining cooperation from informers involves drugs. Many individuals involved in the drug traffic are addicts themselves, and a detective "working" the case will supply his informer with drugs, for his use or to sell, in return for information. The police normally confiscate illegal drugs for evidence, but sometimes hold back a part of the supply to use in paying informers. In some instances, as when they

11

catch a small dealer, and decide to "work" him to gain information, there will be no case, and no paperwork, enabling the police to keep the entire supply for later use.

This is the same method the police use to obtain illegal or unregistered guns. There have been instances of "alibi guns" used by the police to justify a mistaken shooting,[1] and having an untraceable gun to place in the hand of the victim is a prime requirement. A police officer who catches a small criminal on a weapons charge may be inclined to let him go and keep the weapon for himself.

The biggest advantages the police have are the large resources available to them. Despite the fashionable practice among police administrators to cry "poor mouth" to the media, claiming that they're undermanned, under-equipped, and under-funded, they have far more than most citizens do. They have large budgets for expensive and elaborate equipment. Most importantly, the police have the time and the manpower to do a full-scale surveillance. They can assign teams of detectives to the task, depending on its importance.

Oftentimes, the police are clumsy in their efforts. In one instance, a man suspected of child molestation and murder found himself under 24-hour surveillance by the police. The plainclothesmen assigned to the case were so inept that the suspect spotted them repeatedly and, in arrogance and indignation, complained to the press.

It's been fashionable for many decades to say that the police are stupid. This isn't quite true, as their methods are often more due to organizational stupidity and inefficiency than to intellectual defects of individual officers. In any event, they get the job done, more or less. The advantages of their organization outweigh the drawbacks of their methods.

12

They can, for example, assign rotating teams to do 24-hour-a-day surveillance on a subject. These teams are equipped with cars and radios. Often, the police agency has a stock of unmarked cars, seized and confiscated, to use for surveillance.

If the surveillance team needs binoculars, they need only draw them from the supply room. If they need a low-light scope, chances are the department has some in stock, or can borrow one from another agency. The devices a private citizen must go out of his way to get are commonly available to a police agency.

If there's a need for photographic surveillance, the police have not only the cameras and the film, but trained specialists to do the actual photography if the detectives working the case can't do it themselves. If a detective takes some photographs, he never needs to go inside a darkroom, and he can have the photographs processed on a rush basis, even at night in some agencies. Of course, he doesn't pay for this from his own pocket.

The police can man a wiretap on the same 24-hour-a-day basis, and sometimes still do, despite the availability of automatic recording equipment which reduces the need for manpower.

The police have file systems to keep track of suspects and of people even tangentially connected with investigations. State police organizations have computers into which local agencies can tap to aid their investigations. The Department of Justice has the National Crime Information Computer, available to all agencies wired in to it.

To aid in undercover work, the police can call on the cooperation of other, non-police agencies, to provide false documentation for their agents. Private citizens have no such resources.

Some industries have organized their own proprietary information services. The insurance industry, for example, has been victimized by con artists perpetrating insurance frauds. Its members regularly check claims against the information in the central computer, to find out if the claimant has made a claim before.

Thus we see that the police have powers beyond the reach of Joe Citizen. We also see that private organizations, by employing huge staffs and buying very expensive equipment, can build record-keeping facilities that aid them greatly in their investigations.

What, then, can the average citizen do? A working man doesn't have the lavish expense account or sophisticated equipment of these official and semi-official agencies. In the next chapter, we'll take a look at the advantages that the private citizen has over the police, if he's astute enough to use them.

Sources

1. *No Second Place Winner*, William Jordan, Privately printed, copyright 1965, pp. 15-17.

WHAT CAN
THE PRIVATE CITIZEN DO?

The ordinary citizen lacks the resources of the police and other agencies. He usually has to work a job, and can only do surveillance in his off-hours, such as evenings, weekends, and vacations. He also must pay all of his expenses out of his own pocket, lacking taxpayers' dollars to foot the bill. This limits his methods and schedules.

The picture is not entirely discouraging, because the private citizen has open to him certain advantages that agencies lack:

Familiarity

In surveillance and stake-outs, familiarity with the territory is an asset. The private citizen often knows his neighborhood and workplace much better than any outsider, even a police officer. He knows where every window and door is, who lives where, who is home and at what times, which is useful background information for planning a surveillance.

Special Knowledge

Often, he has more knowledge of his subject than any police investigator could. The subject may be a fellow worker, an employee, or a relative. The private citizen has a "feel" for the subject denied to a stranger. This comes about through long-term familiarity, denied to an investigator. The professional gets in and gets out, because he has a caseload to work, not just one individual. He can't take the time to understand every facet of the case, and often must make snap judgements because the caseload is pressing him. The private citizen can pursue the matter at his leisure.

Access

In certain cases, the private citizen lives in the same home, as in the case of an unfaithful spouse. He doesn't need a search warrant to "toss" the premises, as the police do, or a court order to plant a bug.

Also in certain instances, the private citizen normally has access to the place he needs to enter. This enables him to do a surreptitious search, if he gets the opportunity. At least, he won't arouse suspicion by his presence.

Enlisting Willing Help

The private citizen can also enlist the informal cooperation of others, in instances where he has the leverage. For example, an employer worried about theft or industrial espionage can enlist an employee to spy for him, or out of company loyalty. Sometimes, it's possible to enlist aid out of sympathy, as in the case of surveillance of a spouse. Friends will sometimes help.

While Joe Citizen doesn't have quite the coercive power of the police, as he can't put a "twist" on someone he wants as an accomplice or informer, the high quality of the help more than makes up for lack of quantity. He gets willing helpers, not sullen and resentful ones as do the police when they develop informers.

The Law

Both the police and the private citizen are subject to the same laws governing illegal entry, wiretapping, invasion of privacy, etc., but the citizen has more latitude. His actions are not subject to the same scrutiny as police investigations, and he does not have to file a report on everything he does. This frees him from the need to falsify official documents, as some police officers do to cover up illegal aspects of an investigation.

The police run their surveillance with the purpose of building towards a prosecution. Under the "discovery" rule, they must, in a criminal case, make their evidence available to the defense, and in any event, it comes out in court. Any illegally obtained evidence is subject to "exclusion," which means the police must be very circumspect about what they do, or at least be able to cook up another explanation for the evidence they obtained by illegal means, in order for the case to stand up in court. Often, they must perjure themselves to appear to be on the straight and narrow, covering up a lead obtained illegally.

The citizen usually does not aim towards a climax in court. Informal evidence is enough for his purposes, and he does not have the court watchdog peering over his shoulder. While he can still run into bad luck, and be caught and prosecuted if he does something illegal, he's under no obligation to prepare for a courtroom presentation, and consequently his only concern is getting caught in the normal course of affairs. Burglary and certain other surveillance techniques are illegal, and he must be watchful. Unfortunately, if he gets caught, he can be prosecuted.

Joe Citizen can do a lot. Everything depends on how well he uses the advantages he has.

TAILING ON FOOT

This is the most demanding form of surveillance. It's more an art than a science, because it depends on skill, not on equipment. It's hard to follow a subject for many hours without arousing his suspicion. The subject may also board a bus, train, or aircraft, which will place a severe demand on the resourcefulness of the tailer.

Preparations

There are several essential steps to take before starting on any tailing. The first step is to have a clear idea of the type of tail. A *loose tail* is following from a distance, with the emphasis on remaining unseen. There's the risk of losing the subject, but the priority is that he remains unaware of the tail.

A *close tail* runs the risk of detection and is used when it is essential not to lose the subject.

A *rough tail* is one without any precautions against detection. The subject may be aware that you're in the area, and may even be cooperative, as in the case of an undercover agent followed by backup observers.

Practical planning includes the following:

(1) It's essential to know the geography of the area thoroughly. This is easier to say than to do. A tail can start in one locale and finish in another, even another city across the country.

Knowing the area involves more than studying a map. It means knowing bus depots, restaurants, airline terminals, the subway system if there is one, and also knowledge of danger spots, where the subject may lose the tail. These include hotels and other buildings with more than one exit through which the subject may duck while his tail is outside, waiting for him to re-emerge.

A personal reconnaissance of the area before starting the tail is essential, in order to select vantage points for observation. It's often necessary to stay put while the subject is indoors, and lurking in a doorway for lack of planning is risky.

(2) Knowing everything possible about the subject is important. Among the facts needed are the names and addresses of his relatives and friends, his habits, hangouts, and other information which can suggest his whereabouts at a certain time. This is important in case of loss of contact, as it may be possible to deduce where he's going, to pick him up again there. And of course, every member of the team should know what the subject looks like.

(3) Physical preparations include having the right clothing to fit in with the locale. A shadower in a three-piece suit will stand out in a working-class neighborhood. It's also vital to plan for a change of profile, a primitive but effective means of disguise, to impede recognition if the subject watches behind himself.

(4) Having money and credit cards on hand is important, in case the subject takes a taxi, airplane, or

other public transport. A supply of coins helps if it's necessary to make a call from a pay phone.

(5) If there's more than one shadower, they should plan the tail in advance, to decide such questions as who follows whom if the subject makes contact with another person. Designating a team leader is vital, because there may be a need to make an impromptu decision, such as breaking off the tail if there's too great a risk of detection.

(6) Deciding on a means of communication will help during the operation. This may be hand signals or radios, if available.[1]

(7) A backup system will help, if available. This can be additional shadowers following in a car some distance to the rear. These can relieve the tailers periodically, both to give them rest and minimize the chances of detection.

The Techniques and Tactics of Tailing

Physical appearance plays a role. Anyone who plans to shadow another should have a commonplace appearance, and not stand out in a crowd because of height, weight, or any conspicuous physical characteristics. He should also dress inconspiciously, avoiding bright colors, among other things.

Avoiding eye contact with the subject is important at this stage, but don't look away suddenly. Following from across the street helps to avoid this problem.

Boarding public transport imposes a severe problem for the lone shadower. If the subject's taking a bus or train just to get where he's going, it's not too bad. If you see him waiting for a bus, you may choose to board ahead of him, to avoid giving the impression that you're behind him. Taking a seat at the rear will keep you out of his sight. This is a situation where having money for the exact fare is helpful.

A common trick to detect or ditch surveillance is for the subject to board a bus, wait near the door, and jump off at the last second, leaving any tail stranded on board. If this happens, the only thing to do is to go to the next stop, and wait for the next bus or train. The subject may be on board. Scrambling to get off along with the subject will blow the tail.

Entering a building with several exits. This, too, can be innocent, or a tactic to ditch you. If you can find a place from which to cover all the exits, you might choose to stay outside. If not, following him in is your only choice.

This situation places you in a dilemma. The subject may enter, then turn around and go back out immediately, to see who follows him out.

The building may be a hotel, store, or restaurant. If it's necessary to enter, watch for what the subject does. If it's a restaurant and he orders a meal, order something that you can have served more quickly, and leave before he does, breaking your profile outside before picking him up again. You do run the risk of losing him, if you can't watch all the exits. This is where having a team is very helpful. The ability to cover all the exits can ensure success without risk.

Elevators. We've already taken a quick look at this one, but there's an additional point to note. If you know enough about the subject, you may know his destination. He may have an office on a certain floor, or his stockbroker or doctor may be there. Unless you know this, you might want to board with him, getting off on the same floor but going in the opposite direction and entering another office.

This is where a slight ability to fake people out is useful. Upon entering the other office, you can ask for someone, making up a name. The receptionist will tell you there's nobody there by that name, you'll excuse yourself politely and leave, perhaps in time to see where your subject goes. Use the time in the office to break your profile, taking off a hat or coat. If it's an apartment house, ringing a bell and pretending to be a salesman will consume a few seconds.

Changing pace. The subject may speed up and slow down alternately, to see who keeps pace with him. The worst thing to do is to match his pace. Cross the street and try to keep an eye on him from there. A team can bracket him, defeating this tactic.

A variant on this theme is that the subject may start running quickly. This makes it impossible for the lone shadower to follow without detection. A back-up team with a car can easily cope with this, though.

Confrontation. It occasionally happens that the subject will turn and accuse his shadower. This won't happen if he doesn't detect you. If it does happen, all you can do is deny it, and break off the tail. If you have a team, another member can take up the tail.

The convoy. This is the subject's own loose tail, a confederate who follows him to see if there are any additonal shadowers. This puts the lone shadower at a severe disadvantage. It's necessary to remain very alert to detect a convoy.

The proper response is to shadow the convoy instead of the subject. However, the subject may have an arrangement with his convoy to break in different directions at some point, which makes the possibility of losing the subject very great.

Making a contact. This puts the trailer in a dilemma if he's alone. He might want to know who the contact is, but he can't follow them both when they split. It's important to set priorities in advance. This is where a team is helpful. A compromise solution is to take a photograph of the two, if it's possible to do so without being noticed.

Sometimes a subject will drop a piece of paper to see if anyone picks it up. A lone shadower mustn't fall for this tactic. The rear man of a team can retrieve that paper without being seen.

Taking a route down an empty street or across an uncrowded open area is a common tactic to check for a tail. This is a difficult situation, because it means dropping so far back that you might lose sight of the subject. The subject may remain concealed at the other side, to see if anyone follows him across.

One way to handle this is to go around the area, if possible. Taking a parallel street or a route around the open field may let you close in with the subject and keep him in sight. It will probably be necessary to run, though. This is where a back-up team with a car can cope.

Ambush. Some subjects will stop around a corner or doorway and ambush a shadower. This is an unavoidable risk, as sometimes it's necessary to follow a subject closely enough to open yourself up to an ambush. Having a team helps here, too. Some forewarning is possible, if you know that your subject has a history of violence.

Team Tailing

This is by far the better method if you have the manpower. This enables someone else to take over to avoid the risk that the subject will notice the same person behind him all the time.

Usually, the team operates in a loose formation. A two-person team will use the A and B formation. "A"

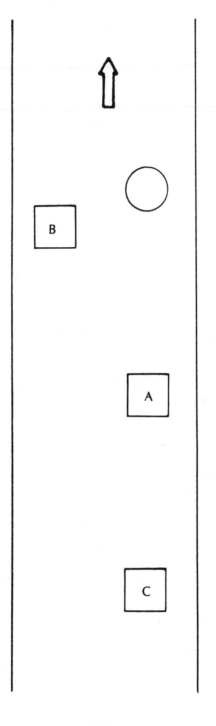

Figure 1

stays behind the subject, while "B" stays farther behind, keeping "A" in sight but out of sight of the subject. Periodically, they rotate.

Another A and B formation is to work opposite sides of the street, with "B" on the opposite side and a little ahead or behind. See Figure 1.

The formations must be loose and flexible, to enable the members to change places smoothly if the subject stops or changes direction.

A three-person team offers more advantages. There's one more relief to minimize the chances of detection. This team also walks in formation, with "A" closest to the subject, "B" across the street, and "C" further behind "A." They will have rehearsed ways to keep close to the subject and rotate places regularly, without becoming conspicuous.

If the subject changes direction, "A" crosses the street and takes the place occupied by "B." "C" closes in, and "B" takes "C"'s place. See Figure 2. The point is to enable a smooth transition, without any member having either to stop or break into a run.

A female member of the team helps immeasurably, as this is a very effective method of avoiding the subject's becoming aware of a tail.

If the subject makes several turns around corners to see if anyone's following, a team that can change formations will avoid being spotted. A team's also more useful if there's a convoy. The lead person, "A," can concentrate on following the subject, while "B" can look out for the convoy.

A team's also incomparably superior in case of a confrontation or an ambush. In a confrontation, "A" can simply break off, leaving "B" and "C" to follow, and in an ambush, having the additional fighting power can save "A" from serious injury.

26

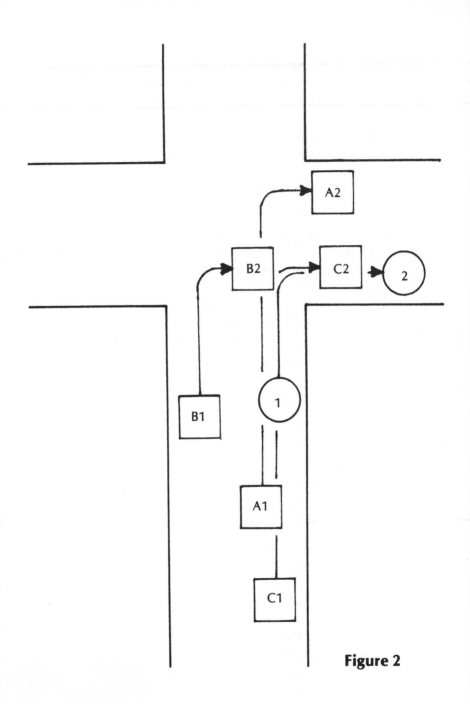

Figure 2

27

Radio contact gives additional flexibility, as one or more members can walk on parallel streets, or stay very far back so as to be utterly out of sight, but not out of reach.

Following by car often gives even greater flexibility, and we'll cover this in the next chapter.

Sources

1. Inexpensive radios are very helpful. One such is the "Easy Talker," available by mail order and advertised in sporting and survivalist magazines. A more powerful walkie-talkie is the Radio Shack TRC-212, a five-watt, forty-channel pocket set with optional hand mike and earphone, which are important. Holding the radio up to talk or listen can be conspicuous. The list price is $139.95.

AUTOMOBILE TAILING

Surveillance by automobile is more difficult for the lone operator than foot tailing. The action happens faster, and there are more opportunites for losing the subject because the shadower must both pay attention to his driving and the demands of keeping close contact.

Preparation

As in foot tailing, adequate preparation can make it or break it. Knowing all you can find out about your subject and the area is important. The make and license number of his car will be necessary. His driving habits and ability will make a difference.

If, for example, your subject takes short trips to the same places at sedate speeds every day, your job will be easier than if he's a fast, erratic, and unpredictable driver who never visits the same place twice.

You should be a good driver, equipped with a good car. This doesn't mean a car suited for high-speed chases, because if your subject detects you and tries to flee, you've failed at half the job. Rather, your car

29

should be mechanically reliable, so you won't be forced to discontinue a tail because of a breakdown.

Your car should be inconspicuous, which usually means a car of a make and age that's common in your area. Buckwalter[1] suggests that an American car is best, but this isn't necessarily so. It depends on the locale, as in some areas there are many foreign cars on the street. A foreign car is more nimble, smaller, and therefore less conspicuous if the area has many foreign cars.

You may have a serious problem if your subject knows you and your car. In this case, you can consider renting or borrowing another one. One supposed advantage to renting a car is that this makes the plate numbers untraceable to you, if your subject "makes" the car.[2] This isn't necessarily so, because the rental agency will have your name and address, as you're usually required to provide this information and show your drivers license. It's possible to fake this, by appropriate falsification of documents, but then it'll also be necessary to set up a cover identity to open a bank account to get a credit card, and this may be too much trouble.

Another suggestion has been to use special headlights for night driving. These "blackout lights" are shielded, so they don't project a beam forward or to the side, and only illuminate the road in front of the car.[3] The problem with these is installing them on a car that's not yours. The same goes for switches to turn lights on and off, to mask the appearance of the car at night.

Another problem with blackout lights is that, although they're invisible from the front and sides, the beam they project downwards suddenly becomes visible in smoke or fog. Many of these gadgets don't work as well as some people think, and there's no substitute for skill and luck.

30

An important piece of equipment to have is a pair of binoculars, because you may have to make a temporary stationary surveillance while keeping at a distance. Almost any will do, but some are better than others.

A good compromise between quality and price is the Simmons 7 x 42, which sells for between $135 and $150, and gives good low-light performance. They're compact, which means less conspicuous when you raise them to your eyes. Another good type, at more than twice the price, is the Bausch and Lomb Discoverer, 7 x 50, which gives even better low-light performance. Both of these have enough eye relief to permit use with eyeglasses by folding back the rubber caps, and the Bausch and Lombs are slightly better for this purpose than the Simmons. Binoculars become doubly useful when you have a partner to use them.

If possible, have a partner in the car with you. This is more important than when on foot, because there's more to watch, and your attention will be divided. Your partner gives you an additional capacity if your subject parks and enters a building, as he can jump out and follow, while you'd have to find a parking spot first if you were alone. Another advantage is if the subject takes a public conveyance. Your partner can board with him, while you follow with the car. If the subject plays games, such as jumping on and then quickly jumping off, you won't be thrown off as easily as if you were alone.

The choice of partner can affect your success. Keep in mind that a two-man team is conspicuous, and fits perfectly with the movie stereotypes people are accustomed to seeing. A male-female team is better.

Starting Up

How you begin a moving surveillance can determine the success or failure of the project. Real life is not like the movies, where the following car is parked across the street and starts up as soon as the subject moves out. This is too conspicuous, and only a subject who's deaf, dumb, and blind might fail to notice a car with two occupants parked near his premises.

Parking down the block, or farther, with a good pair of binoculars reduces the risk. The geography may help you in this regard. If your subject's on a one-way street, he's not likely to go anywhere but the legal direction, especially if he starts up with no possible surveillant in sight. With luck, you might be able to park out of sight and even around a corner if it's a long, curving street.

Moving With The Subject

The main effort is to keep up with the subject, one or two cars behind him, neither overtaking him nor falling too far behind. It's important never to appear fully in his rear-view mirror to avoid recognition. Keeping one or two cars interposed will help a lot. See Figure 3. Positions "X," "Y," or "Z" are suitable for surveillance.

The distance will vary, depending on the traffic, and whether the area is urban or rural. Dense city traffic has bumper-to-bumper vehicles, stop lights, and one-way streets. This makes it easier for you to lose contact with the subject, even inadvertently. Keeping one or two cars behind will mean an overall distance of perhaps forty feet.

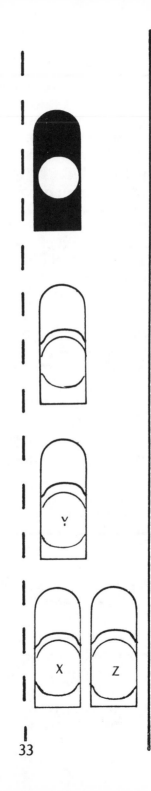

Figure 3

In rural areas, with few cars on the road, you'll have to keep an interval of perhaps hundreds of yards to avoid being spotted. You'll have good visibility though, and your subject will find it harder to shake you.

Keeping in the subject's "blind spot" is usually good practice, if the situation permits. This can only work in city traffic and on streets and roads that have more than one lane. The sector to the subject's right rear is usually the one in which he has the least visibility, because it is not covered by his rearview mirror or left-hand sideview mirror. If he has a rearview mirror on both sides, as some vehicles do, he'll be able to see into this quadrant.

Noting if the subject is alone or has a companion is important, as is careful observation of what the companion does. If he or she turns his head every few seconds, there's no doubt that he's checking for a tail. That doesn't mean he's detected you, but it does give warning to be careful.

Breaking the Profile

While it's impossible to change a vehicle's appearance totally while on a surveillance, there are some subtle actions that can reduce the sense of familiarity if the subject sees it several times in his rearview mirror. Apart from never coming up directly behind him, you can change the silhouettes of yourself and your partners, as well as the car, by some simple tricks.

If the car's a convertible, raising and lowering the top at intervals will help break the profile. You and your partners can put on and remove caps or hats. Your partner can crouch down in the seat at times to make it seem that you're alone if the subject takes a casual look in his mirror.

34

Crouching down and changing positions works even better if you have more than one partner in the car. Having a male-female team in the front seat at one point, and two males at another, will change the appearance of your car in the subject's rearview mirror. You can use any necessary stops for this game of musical chairs.

Tactics

You'll have to have various pre-planned moves to be able to keep up with your subject, as there are many ways of losing contact in traffic. Good tactics will help to minimize your problems, but they're not the whole answer. There's also luck, which every authority on the subject chooses to ignore.

A large vehicle can break down immediately in front of you on a narrow street, cars backed up behind you prevent your moving out and taking another street, and your subject becomes lost. An accident can put you out of action. Your car can break down.

It's true that careful preparation can minimize the chances of something unlucky happening, and enable you to recover more quickly in case it does, but in some instances something will go wrong in spite of everything you can do.

Coping with the moves the subject makes, though, is mainly good tactics, as well as careful observation. Getting a "feel" of how he drives, and learning to anticipate his moves will make a big difference in the minute-by-minute task of following him.

If your subject turns a corner, he might simply be changing direction. At the outset, you might want to pull over before reaching the corner while your partner jumps out to see if the subject has continued, or parked and is waiting for a shadower to turn the corner with him. This delay is possible only when the pace of traffic permits catching up to the subject after starting up again. In most instances, you'll have to turn the corner behind the subject and take your chances.

There are two ways for a single-car shadow to cope with a subject who stops after turning a corner. One is to go beyond him, find a place to pull in, and stop. This gives a good opportunity to change the position of people in the shadowing car. The second way is to go into the intersection slowly, and if the partner calls out that he sees the subject stopped, keep going straight, making the turn on the next block. This means losing sight of the subject for a minute, but as he's stopped, the risk of losing contact is not great. From the parallel street it's simple to make another turn to park on the cross-street ahead of the subject car, picking him up again when he starts to move.

Occasionally, there's a convenience market or gas station on the corner, which will enable you to cross private property to the cross-street, emerging behind the subject's car without having visibly made the turn. If you're lucky enough to have such a feature when your subject makes a turn, by all means use it.

Cutting through a parking lot to make a turn is illegal in some areas, as businessmen have complained of cars cutting across their property to avoid the inconvenience of red lights. Another problem is that of a congested parking lot, where the risk of an accident is much greater than on the street.

If the subject turns up a one-way street, trying to follow him up the one-way will definitely expose you to detection. You'll have to go to the next parallel street to continue the shadow. When you do so, remember there's a 50% chance the subject will turn in your direction after leaving that block, which makes picking him up again much easier.

If the subject makes a left turn as the light turns red, trying to follow him can be both conspicuous and dangerous. It's much better to make a right turn, blend in with the traffic, and make a U-turn as soon as possible. Another possibility is to cut through a shopping center parking lot or that of a gas station, if one happens to be conveniently on your left as you come to the red light.

Following a subject who crosses the intersection, while keeping in a straight line, as the light turns red can be a problem. Much depends on whether he is able to keep going, or has to stop at the next intersection for a red light himself. If you're on a street with staggered lights, he may be caught on the next block, and the light will flash green again for you before it does for him, enabling you to take a station behind him at your leisure.

If not, you many have to make a quick right, then a U-turn, and then another quick right to get back on the street behind him.

If your subject enters a parking lot, what you do will depend heavily on the local situation. One possible tactic is to go in by another entrance, taking up a position from which you can observe him and start up on his track quickly. If the parking lot is small, and you can see it all from the street, there's no need to go in after him. You can simply park down the block, or even pull into another parking lot across the street, if there is one.

If your subject runs a red light, and there's heavy traffic preventing you from following, you may have to admit he's spotted you and give up the tail. There are few situations which require sticking with him at all costs.

You'll also have to admit there are some situations which you won't be able to handle with a one-car tail.

Working Hard

Shadowing is hard work, and makes great demands on both you and your partner, if you have one. You have to be very alert, to avoid losing your subject. You also have to do some things which you would not ordinarily do.

Your partner must keep his eyes glued to the subject, to give you leads regarding his actions. You're watching the road, and can't give your full attention to the task of following. In effect, you'll be taking orders from your partner, and you should be prepared for this.

Your partner's observations are even more important at night, when the subject may make a sudden turn without signalling and may even turn his lights off, to avoid giving you a clue regarding his intention. Your attention will be distracted, and you may easily miss the moment when the subject douses his lights. Only your partner's close attention will prevent losing the subject.

If you stop because your subject has stopped, you should get out of the car and check your tires, giving them a quick eyeball. This is usually excessive attention in normal driving, but when you can't afford to lose your subject because of a flat, it's very important. This also gives you an ostensible reason for stopping, if the subject happens to look your way. If you need more time, check under the hood. This is good general practice, as you must keep the car in top shape every moment.

If you have to park for a short while, observing your subject is not enough. Your partner can keep his eyes on your subject, but as you are momentarily free from having to pay attention to the road, you should be scanning the entire area. Your subject may have pulled into a parking lot to meet someone, and if that someone approaches from your direction and passes you, while you and your partner are intently surveilling the subject with binoculars, that will give it away. If there's a meeting planned, there may be a signal between the two to break off the meeting, or the second party may simply break away on his own and without informing the subject, to avoid being spotted.

If someone approaches your parked car, it's important not to be seen making an obvious surveillance. As a last resort, get out of the car, lock up, and walk away.

If you can, park at a gas station. While it goes without saying that you should begin a shadow with a full tank, topping up during the trip is important. You don't always know how far the tail will take you, and it's possible the subject's vehicle has greater range than yours. Many campers and pick-up trucks, for example, have auxiliary tanks which give them far greater range than most passenger cars.

As noted later in the section on stake-outs, this is also a good time to use the toilet, which can become an almost unbearable problem on long surveillances.

Sources

1. *Surveillance and Undercover Investigation*, Art Buckwalter, Woburn, MA, Butterworth Publishers, 1983, p. 58.
2. *Ibid.*, p. 58.
3. *Ibid.*, p. 59.

AUTOMOBILE SURVEILLANCE PART II

Multiple Car Surveillance

Using more than one car solves many problems, but it brings up a couple of others. Being able to rotate the lead car in a surveillance operation lessens the chances of the subject's noticing the same car behind him mile after mile, and the ability to keep other cars on parallel streets avoids his being out of sight for more than a few seconds when he makes a turn.

If you're lucky enough to have a few friends who are willing to help you out in a moving surveillance, you'll find it necessary to coordinate closely with them to make it a smooth operation, and to avoid tripping over each other.

There are several areas to coordinate, and one new problem. It's necessay to plan tactics and timing, as well as the composition of the team in the cars. The new problem is communication between the cars.

A planning meeting before starting out is essential, and this is the time to settle the tactics and procedures, not later on the road. You'll have to brief your teams on the task, sharing all of your information regarding the subject with them. Often, you make or break the operation at the briefing, and many basically simple operations have become hopelessly snarled because of poor briefing.

The briefing provides the opportunity to hand out maps of the area, find out from your people how well they know the area, decide who will be the drivers and who the riders, distribute necessary equipment, and arrange schedules, if possible.

A lot of the planning involves operationally marginal details, such as arranging for meeting times, lunch breaks, having enough money and credit cards available to meet immediate expenses, and the other primarily administrative matters that can snowball into serious problems if neglected.

Arranging a rendevous point is simple, in principle, and setting a time requires leaving a margin of safety for latecomers. There must be enough time for a last-minute briefing, to coordinate all the activities.

Everybody must understand that everything must be subordinated to the task of keeping the subject in sight. This can be extremely demanding if there's only one car available, but with several the pressure is greatly alleviated. Even assuming, for example, that the subject starts out on a long trip, not stopping for lunch or even for fuel, the shadowers can arrange to stop in relays. One car can stop to pick up sandwiches, and catch up with the others.

It's also possible to handle the problems of fuel and toilet stops by anticipating them and planning. Carrying jerricans of gas in the trunk is one possible solution. The problem of coordinating widely separated cars requires radio contact, and planning for this is essential.

Communications

There are basically two ways of communicating between vehicles: visible signals, and radio. Visible signals are the cheap way to do it, but this requires that the vehicles be within sight of each other. Hand signals are harder to see in darkness. If you plan to use the very effective methods of keeping one or more vehicles on parallel streets, you'll have to use radio.

CB is very popular, and many people have CB sets, either portable walkie-talkies, or installed in their vehicles. If you and your team already have CBs, you'll be familiar with the equipment's limitations. If not, and you plan to buy some, you can spend a lot of money on unneeded equipment, and even buy radios that are not the best for the task. Let's run down the qualities that CB equipment must have for this purpose:

It must be affordable. Goverment agencies can buy portable radios that cost two thousand dollars each, but individuals have a harder time of it.

It should cover all forty channels. The lower twenty-three channels of the original CB standard are the crowded ones, and you'll probably find the upper channels with less traffic.

The radios should tune by means of phase-locked loop circuitry, not crystals. Crystals are all right for radios that accept only one or two channels, but buying crystals for all forty CB channels will cost more than the radio itself.

The power supply should be both plug-in to the car's system via the cigarette lighter, and internal batteries. It helps, but is not always essential, to have the set portable, in case it's necessary to take it out of the car as when doing a foot reconnaissance.

The internal batteries should be easily replaceable. Running out of juice during an operation can cause a

42

serious problem. The batteries may be nicad, as these are more economical during the long run because they're rechargable. However, you should be aware of the fact that nicads deliver both lower voltage and less life per charge than ordinary dry cells. An average figure is 40% of the life of standard dry cells. Unfortunately, nicads have been oversold by intense advertising, which never mentions that they have short intervals between recharges. Alkaline and other long-life cells last much longer than zinc-carbon dry cells.

If you have nicads, you can get away with using them by running off the car's power supply to save draining them, and having a set of conventional spares in case you need to be out of the car for a long time. Keep in mind that transmitting drains the batteries much more quickly than receiving.

Some specific equipment you might consider, if you don't already have the CB sets you need, are the following:

The KRACO "Mayday II" sells for between sixty and ninety dollars, depending on the store and whether or not there's a sale on. This is an emergency radio set that comes in a fitted plastic carrying case. It's a light, portable unit that contains its own batteries and has a plug for the cigarette lighter, to save the batteries when operating in the car. There are two antennas, a rubber duck and an outside antenna that clamps magnetically to the car roof. Either one works, but the outside antenna gives greater range, up to two miles under good conditions. The tuning is phase-locked loop, for all forty channels. It takes ten "A" cells.

The Radio Shack TRC-412 is similar in price and weight, but it operates only on the car's power supply and the roof antenna. This makes it less versatile.

At a higher price, there's the Radio Shack TRC-212, a five-watt portable with phase-locked loop tuning for all forty channels. This has more options than the KRACO, at extra cost. One of the options is a battery charger, for use with nicads. Another is the hand mike.

A CB that's designed for permanent installation is the Radio Shack TRC-473, at $139.95. This is the conventional CB layout, and it's necessary to buy a roof antenna at extra cost for this unit. It requires drilling some holes and hooking up wires.

More important than the equipment is method of use. Anyone who uses a radio must understand that he's speaking for the world to hear, and that especially on the CB there are many ears listening. Transmissions must be short and discreet.

Discretion means not giving away information to anyone who may be listening. Don't use any names, just designations such as "Car A," "Car B," etc. Avoid using the subject's name. Refer to him only as "the subject," or "Mr. A." It's also helpful not to be too explicit in passing on messages or instructions. Referring to "Plan B" instead of spelling it out will keep listeners in the dark.

Sometimes mentioning place names will be unavoidable. You may find it necessary to announce: "Subject is turning onto Ash Avenue," or the like. To minimize the problem this can cause, have a list of known locations, such as the subject's home, and refer to them only as "Point A," "Point B," etc.

When you or any of your group are on the air, keep an eye on the subject. If he starts turning his head right after one of you mentions a place-name, this suggests very strongly that he's listening in, and that you've just blown it.

Part of being discreet is avoiding heavily-used channels. Not only does this help by reducing the number of listeners, it aids your communications by avoiding having to compete with other traffic. There are several channels to avoid:

Channel 9, the emergency channel.

Channel 14, the walkie-talkie channel. Every kid with a toy radio is shouting on this one.

Channels 17 and 19, the trucker's channels. These are in almost constant use, twenty-four hours a day.

Channel 23, an alternate trucker's channel in some parts of the country. This channel is also the upper end of the old standard, and there are still many CBs that can't go higher than this one.

The channels between 23 and 40 will usually have far less traffic than the lower ones. This means it'll be easier to find one that's free, and less likelihood of running into a "motormouth" who monopolizes the channel. This last part can be a serious problem, and anyone who's listened to the CB knows that some users show extremely bad manners, and often spoil it for the rest.

It will be necessary to change channels regularly, both to find a quiet one, and to evade detection if the subject's a CB user. If he is, the chances are he'll be on channel 19, the most widely used road channel. When calling for a change of channel, have a prepared list, with all the channels designated by letters, not numbers. Anyone listening in won't be able to follow you easily, and will have to search for your traffic.

Avoiding useless chit-chat is another important point. Make sure your people understand the priority of leaving the channel clear for urgent transmissions. This includes not answering anyone not in the group. Sometimes, there's a request for a "radio check" or the like, and ignoring these will help keep the channel clear. The caller will simply assume nobody heard him, and try another channel.

Tactics for Multi-Car Tails

Tailing with more than one car involves the same principles as single-car surveillance, but there are a lot more choices open to the tail. There are also various tactics to keep contact and minimize detection.

The basic tactic is to rotate the lead car regularly to avoid recognition by the subject. There are several ways of doing this. One, useful if there's no radio contact, is simply to drop back and wave another car on. Taking a freeway exit, coming on again, and assuming the tail position is yet another way.

A good point at which to change positions is whenever the subject turns a corner. He may be doing this to check for a tail, and to see the same car following him around each turn will alert him. Keeping several cars behind him may not fool him, and changing positions is a much better way.

If the subject turns into an alley, it may be to park or check for a tail. With only one car, it would be necessary either to take a chance and follow him in, or stop and make a foot reconnaissance before proceeding. With several cars, it's possible to send one to circle around and watch the exit on the next street, without risking being spotted.

If the subject stops around a corner or curve, the lead car can simply pass him, meanwhile alerting the others by radio so that they may stop short of the curve and wait. The lead car continues until there's a convenient place to park, and keeps the subject under observation.

It may not be possible to find a convenient parking spot, and the subject may be watching for this, anyway, if he's sophisticated. This is where having the partner leave the car with a portable radio for a foot reconnaissance is very helpful. It enables the driver to

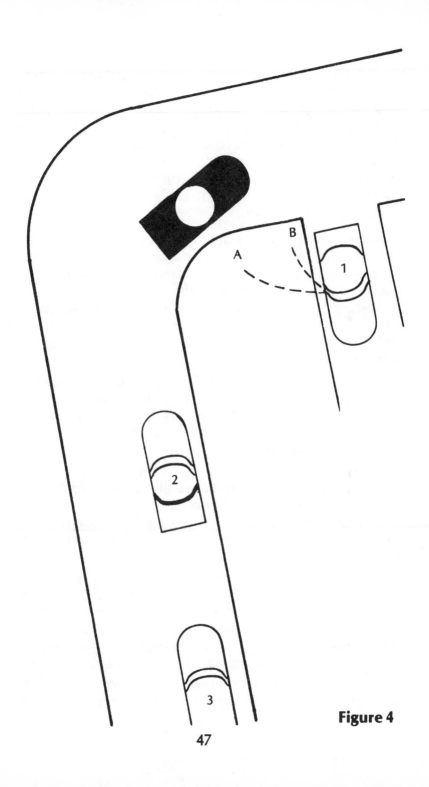

Figure 4

park well out of sight, and the partner on foot can keep in contact with all of them with the radio. He doesn't have to worry about making it back to the car if the subject starts moving again, because the lead car will be last in line this time, to avoid recognition. In Figure 4, we see that the lead car, 1, has parked around the corner, while cars 2 and 3 are stopped before the curve in the road. Someone from car 1 can jump out and watch from concealment at Point A or Point B.

If the subject tries to detect a tail by making a quick U-turn, the lead car continues until it's out of sight before making its U-turn. If there's enough interval between the cars on a multi-car tail, one of the following cars can make a left turn before the subject's car arrives, make a quick U-turn in the block out of sight, then pull out and behind him as if it were making a normal right turn.

Combining car and foot tailing gives great versatility. It's useful when the subject is on foot, and when he parks and leaves his car. Having one or two cars as backup for a foot tail helps if the subject boards public transport, or meets and is picked up by someone in a vehicle.

The multiple-car technique really comes into its own if there are two or more people in the subject car, and they split up. Dividing forces to follow them all is simpler than trying to face the dilemma of whom to follow when there aren't enough people available.

Using more than one car for tailing is a very powerful technique, if you do it properly. It helps overcome some of the problems that bad luck can impose upon you, such as the street between you and your subject being blocked. With another car on a parallel street, it will still be possible to maintain contact. A traffic accident or a breakdown of your car won't put the project out of action.

Tailing at Night

Nightfall brings with it some problems, as well as some relief from other problems. The lower visibility works both ways, as it's harder for the subject to see who's following and the tail has more trouble keeping track of the subject's car.

One thing that helps a lot is to smash one of the subject's tail lights. This works better than a piece of reflective tape,[1] because if the subject notices the broken light, the most logical assumption is that it was broken by someone who was careless in parking behind him.

One problem with tailing at night is that your headlights will be very visible for a long way off. This isn't serious if there's other traffic, as headlights look even more alike than tail lights, but in a rural area they'll give you away. Driving without lights is one way out, but it may attract the attention of the police. Gadgets such as "blackout lights" have the same problem.

In one instance, a police officer drove without lights to catch a speeder, who didn't notice him until the officer lit the rotating beacon on top of his car and pulled him over.[2]

Sources

1. *Surveillance and Undercover Investigation,* Art Buckwalter, Woburn, MA, Butterworth Publishers, 1983, p. 96.
2. The author witnessed this event, which occurred on the New Jersey Turnpike at about four A.M. one spring morning. There was a large Mercury station wagon, bombing down the road at well over the speed limit, its driver complacently unaware that the troopers

occasionally enforced the speed laws. Suddenly, a large black shadow sped by the author's car on the left side, doing at least ninety miles per hour. The shadow slipped into the saddle behind the station wagon, its bulk blotting out the wagon's tail lights, and the trooper stayed in place long enough to "clock" him. Then the patrol car lit up like a merry-go-round, blinkers, cherry-top, and all, and the station wagon slowed and pulled over, the trooper right behind him.

ELUDING A TAIL

If you're being followed, you will want to find out, and perhaps elude the tail. There are many reasons you may be followed, from fairly harmless ones to some that can be very serious for you. If you're a businessman who takes the day's cash to the night drop at the bank, you are prey for a criminal attack.

One obvious way to find out if you're being followed is to look outside before leaving, and notice the people on the street. When you leave, being aware of the people around you is helpful.

You can take some specific steps, without wasting too much time or seeming paranoid. One good rule is not to take the same route each day, if it's a regular trip, and to start at different times. This will help to throw off shadowers.

Another is to stop occasionally, looking at the faces of the people behind you, not their clothing. If you notice that you keep seeing the same face, make a few turns around corners, to see who's following.

Walking across a park or down an isolated street will show up a tail. There's a risk in this, if you fear a criminal attack.

Having someone follow you in turn, a convoy, as discussed earlier, is a very effective method of showing up a tail.

Going into a building and coming out again quickly is another way of discovering a tail. Yet another is to take a bus or subway, to see if anyone boards with you and gets off at the same stop.

Changing your pace, stopping and dawdling, and reversing direction are all ways of checking for a tail. Don't make it obvious, though.

Taking an elevator or escalator will often disclose a shadow if he gets on with you. Going to a specific floor, then coming down again immediately makes it very hard for anyone to follow you unnoticed.

Once you've discovered that you're being followed, you have to decide what to do about it. You may decide that it's safer to pretend you're unaware and allow the shadower to follow you, while you lead him on a wild goose chase. On the other hand, the urgency of the situation may force you to evade him, and there are several good ways of doing this.

Eluding a Tail on Foot

Take a public conveyance, remain near the door, and jump off just before it starts. This method offers you two choices, really. If your tail jumps off with you, you may be able to board again at the last second without his being able to follow you as the doors close. Another way is to make a lunge towards the door, faking him out and inducing him to jump off while you remain behind. Do this several times and you'll lose the tail.

Take the last taxi in a line. Unless you have a team with a car on your tail, you'll shake the shadow.

Use a building with multiple exits, even if they're not public ones. Going into a restaurant, dashing into the kitchen, and leaving through the alley will both disclose anyone following and perhaps lose him if he's not right behind you.

Set up an ambush. This is extreme, but justifiable if you're sure of a criminal attack. Be aware that if you're wrong, you won't have a leg to stand on, legally.

In setting up an ambush, the intent is surprise, which can compensate for not having a weapon. You'll want to find a spot where you can have privacy for a few seconds, to dispose of the tail and not have witnesses identifying you to the police. This is critically important, because even if you're certain the shadower is a mugger, until he attacks you he's just another innocent citizen, and you'll be liable for assault and battery.

The second important point about an ambush is attaining surprise. You must be out of sight of your tail for a few seconds while you take a hiding place. This means going into a building, around a corner, or a bend in the road.

Set up the ambush around the corner, or in an elevator, or parking garage. Any place that enables you to surprise the shadower will do. A public restroom is another choice, if he follows you in.

A good idea is to select a spot where the light will throw his shadow as he approaches, giving you warning to get set.

Don't give your shadower an even break. Use a weapon. He may be armed, and your best chance is to put him down quickly. If you carry a briefcase, that may be your weapon. Otherwise, improvise. A tire iron, a two-by-four, or piece of heavy pipe will be excellent. If you're skilled at unarmed combat, you may feel you don't need a weapon.

A gun isn't the best choice. You may not own one, or may not be carrying it if you do. A gun is noisy, and silencers are both ineffective and grossly illegal, as well as hard to get.

Choosing where to strike depends on your purpose. If you have an urgent need to disable the tail, and get where you're going, staying low and striking for his knees will put him down and keep him from following you. The advantage of this method is that you don't risk killing him.

If you're certain the shadower is out to harm you, strike for the face or solar plexus, putting all your weight behind the blow. As he starts to go down, another blow to the back of the head will help assure that he stays down.

Tear gas sprays are unreliable. Spraying your shadower's face may incapacitate him, or if he's resistant, it may make him mad, and you'll have to fight him.

A staircase is an excellent locale for an ambush, especially if it's an enclosed fire stair. Pushing someone down a flight of stairs is simple, and can result in severe injury to the person taking the fall. Best of all, it can look like an "accident," and your shadow's not likely to press charges if he survives.

A non-violent way of physically stopping a tail is possible in some situations. If you know the area, and can lead your shadow through a building which has an exit you can lock from the outside after passing through, you'll stop him cold. Sometimes, it's possible simply to shove a chair under the doorknob.

If there's more than one shadower, as in the case of a group of muggers, trying to fight or disable them isn't likely to succeed. There are then only two choices: blocking and confrontation, if you can't get to safety.

Blocking an exit is one way, if you can be sure that one hasn't circled around to be able to follow you. Confrontation is the other way, and usually requires a gun.

"Drawing down" on a group of muggers is effective, if you can catch them bunched up, to avoid being attacked from the rear or side. Showing a weapon, especially if you can give the impression that you're willing and able to use it, will discourage them, and let you out of the situation.

Eluding an Automobile Tail

Generally, it's easier to detect and evade a tail by a car than it is on foot. The reason is that vehicles are much more limited in their actions, and you can take advantage of this very easily, as we shall see.

The simplest way to detect a tail is to avoid going directly to your destination. Take several turns, watching for cars that follow you. Going through four right-angle turns will usually be enough to show a tail, as people normally don't drive in circles.

It's very helpful to have another person in the car when seeking to detect a tail. You have to keep your eyes and mind on your driving, and dividing your attention will reduce your effectiveness. This is why an observer is helpful.

Another way is to vary your speed. Speed up, then slow down. Watch for cars that don't pass you when you're going slowly. This will show up vehicles that are keeping pace with you.

Yet another way is to drive at a very low speed, forcing other cars to pass you and watching for cars that either stay behind you or park and start up again.

Turn a corner and park. Watch for anyone who stops with you. This is also a good way of eluding a tail, especially at night. Parking, turning the engine and lights off, and lying down on the seat may enable you to avoid discovery. This works best if you're driving fast and the follower has to drive at high speed to keep up with you. If you park and douse your lights, unseen around a corner, and if there's other traffic, he'll probably be so intent on looking forward, and traveling so fast, that he'll probably miss you.

Going the wrong way up a one-way street is a sure way of exposing anyone who follows you. Unfortunately, you can only do this when there's very little traffic.

Making a sudden U-turn is another way of detecting a tail. Anyone who turns and follows you will be visible in your rear-view mirror.

In any locale where there are traffic lights, you can not only detect, but "shake" a tail by making it look accidental. Time the lights, adjusting your speed so you arrive at a light just when it's flashing yellow. This will make it harder for your tail to go through, especially if he's a few cars back.

Many surveillants will keep one or more cars back to avoid being prominent in their subject's rear-view mirror. This helps concealment, but makes it harder for them to follow the subject's maneuvers. At a red light, the shadower may want to take a chance and go through, but the car in front will block him.

Driving into a dead-end street is another way of showing up a tail, but the drawback is that if he's about to attack you, you'll be boxed in. In any event, the moment you come out of the cul-de-sac, he'll pick you up again, if he's done the smart thing and waited for you outside.

There are "bumper beepers" available, and someone might have stuck one on your car, permitting tailing without keeping as close as with a visual tail. If you have good reason to believe you're going to be followed, it's worth the trouble to go over your car for one of these. While you're doing that, look for a broken tail light, or other signs that can make your car easier to follow.

In searching your car for a bug, don't do it where you can be seen. Do it inside a garage or courtyard. If a watcher sees you searching, he'll be alert to the prospect of your finding the transmitter, and will be more cautious in shadowing you.

Keep in mind that they're not always obvious. They can be disguised as part of the car. The weak point, and usually the giveaway, is that a bumper beeper requires an antenna. This can be a thin piece of wire up to a foot long, and the sight of one of these hanging under your car is a strong clue that you've been "bugged."

What do you do with it if you find it? The instinctive reaction is to destroy it, but there's a better way. Remember that a transmitter enables a tail to follow you while keeping far enough back as to be out of your sight. A directional receiver in his car will tell him your location.

If he's out of your sight, you're out of his, and you can take advantage of this fact. Go out into traffic, and plant the device on another car. Since many of these beepers are attached by a magnet, it is easy for you to attach them to another car, even one beside you at a stoplight. If there's no magnet, throw it into the back of a pick-up truck. This will lead your tail in another direction.

The Chase

Once you're sure you're being tailed, it's no longer a surveillance, but becomes a chase. The dividing line isn't clear-cut, and some of the actions you take to detect a tail also work to evade a chase, as we've already seen. From this point on, though, we'll consider overt actions that you can take to "ditch" a tail or chase.

These will show your tail that you're aware of him, and may even provoke a violent reaction. Some of them are dangerous, and it's impossible to make a blanket suggestion that will work in all cases.

We'll start out with the less drastic actions. This one's possible only on a freeway, with light to moderate traffic. Stay in the left lane, and drive until an exit comes up. Your tail, with a little luck, will be somewhere behind you in the left lane. If you have a clear shot at the exit, cut across the traffic lanes and take it. Don't use your turn signal, as this would alert your tail. Your tail, by the time he reacts, will have missed the exit.

If he's close behind you, you'll have a good chance of ditching him. If he's been laying back, as he would with light traffic, your chances are much less, as he'll have a chance to react.

This will work in heavy traffic, too, because it often happens that cars bunch up, leaving intervals between groups, and you can use such gaps to make your break. The higher your speed, the better the odds in your favor, because your tail will be likely to be sticking to you more closely, and the speed will give him less time to react.

What works in your favor, even if the traffic is heavy, is that a gap next to you means that there will be cars next to him, blocking his movement. You can exploit this when you make your break.

He might, if he's really desperate, choose to break from the traffic violently and come across the grass to make the exit. This isn't always possible, as many superhighways have low retaining walls or fences to set them off. If you see your tail coming after you nevertheless, your backup plan is to take the on-ramp again, as you'll have gotten a lead on him and a high-speed run will give you a chance of losing him in the traffic.

At night, several quick turns will help you lose a tail. In this case, you want to get a lead of at least a block on him. One way to do this is to slow down, as if checking for a tail. He'll drop back somewhat, to reduce the chances of your seeing him.

At a corner, turn quickly without signalling your intention. This should be easy, because in driving slowly, you'll probably be in the right-hand lane, and taking a quick right will be safe and easy. Don't increase your speed at all until you're completely out of sight, to avoid alerting your tail.

As soon as you're around the corner, accelerate as quickly as you can and douse your lights. If you can make it to the next intersection before he comes around behind you, he won't know in which direction you've turned, and he'll have to think fast when he gets there. At the next corner, turn again, still with your lights out, in case he's in sight.

If you don't have enough of a lead to get to the corner before he comes around behind you, look for an alley. This is where knowing the geography will help you greatly. An alley that lets out onto the next street will give you a free run. A dead-end alley is a trap.

So far, we've looked at passive measures, techniques of ditching rather than stopping. If these don't work, there are more forceful methods available.

Stopping a car by gunfire can work, but it's usually not justifiable, so let's dispose of it here. It's hard to shoot and hit a target from a car, despite what we see on television. In fact, many police agencies forbid their officers from opening fire from a moving car. The risk of hitting innocent people is too high.

Gunfire will only work well if the scene is an isolated road, where there's no danger of hitting innocent people, and when someone other than the driver can do the shooting. Driving a car while shooting backwards is strictly "mission impossible."

If shooting is necessary, the passenger should do it, but keep in mind that opening fire may provoke return fire from the other car. If it's a high-speed chase, shooting for the radiator, rather than the driver, is more likely to get a hit. Increasing speed will force the other to follow suit, thereby putting more of a load on his cooling system.

Disabling the following vehicle by various methods is next. Some of these methods require special equipment, some of which can be improvised.

One way is to pour oil on the pavement while going around a corner. The passenger can do this and the following car will skid out of control, if all goes well. For this to work, it's necessary to be going fast enough so that a slight loss in tire adhesion will cause a disastrous skid. The road surface is important. Asphalt, with its less porous surface, is better than rough concrete or gravel, which will absorb the oil quickly.

It's essential to turn a corner, because a car is much less likely to skid when traveling in a straight line. The nature of the terrain is not as important as it might seem. While sending a pursuer off a cliff is spectacular and final, a much less drastic mishap will stop him. Crashing into a retaining wall can break an axle, or bend the front bumper and fender in far enough to blow a tire or prevent steering. A high-speed crash into a tree or building is usually the end of the road for him.

In the event the pursuer doesn't crash, you'll still cramp his style, as he'll be much more careful in following you around corners, and you'll find it easier to evade him.

Some drug traffickers and moonshiners have oil spray systems in their cars. These consist of an oil reservoir and electric pump controlled by a switch located conveniently on the dashboard, and a set of spray nozzles under the rear bumper. This permits spraying a slick film on the road behind them very quickly to discourage pursuit. Without such a system, it's necessary to pour the oil by hand, which is not as effective.

A slower and less certain method of discouraging pursuit is to use a tear gas spray. Unless the following car is closed up, this will drift into the open window or air intake and affect the driver. It isn't necessary to disable the driver totally, as even some tearing or coughing will impair his ability to keep closely on your tail.

At high speed, a slight bump in the road can impede control of a car, and hitting an object can cause total loss of control and a crash. A relatively small object will do, such as a rock, a metal can, or a piece of wood. Dropping some of these out of a rear door will impede pursuit. The chances are greater of causing a crash at night, but even in daylight when the driver can see the obstacles in the road, he'll have to swerve or slow down to avoid them. This will increase your chances of evasion.

If you keep several two-by-fours in your back seat, your passenger can throw them out so they land across the road, making it difficult for the pursuer to avoid them.

Objects with sharp edges or corners can cause a blowout. A brick, sharp rock, or a specially-manufactured device will work if the tire hits it. One such special device, called a "caltrop," consists of a tetrahedron, a four-pointed affair made of two pieces of steel tubing, each about four inches long, with sharpened ends and bent to about 120 degrees, then welded together. See Figure 5. This always lands with one point up when it comes to rest. The point will puncture any tire that runs over it, and the tube will let the air out.

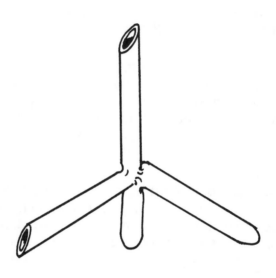

Figure 5

Some of the more spectacular methods, grenades and gasoline bombs, are just not practical, despite what we see on television. Grenades are not commonly available, and using one to stop a car is almost impossible. It's necessary that the car be right over it when it goes off, and this is extremely hard to time accurately.

A gasoline bomb, much easier to obtain, isn't practical for two reasons: the danger of lighting one inside a moving car is prohibitive; and the pursuing car can easily drive through the flames, escaping damage because of the short exposure to fire.

A form of ambush you can set up without weapons or special equipment is to provoke a crash by driving around a corner on a narrow road or street, and leaving your car's back seat in the road. You need enough of a lead so you have time to stop for the few seconds this will take.

In so doing, you have to be sure of placing the seat close enough to the turn so that the driver of the following car doesn't have room to react effectively. If he can brake before hitting it, your action will only delay him slightly. If he's forced to steer into something else to avoid the obstacle, he'll crash.

A desperate but effective measure is to leave your car parked across the road around a corner. This will be impossible to avoid if the road's narrow, and there will be a disabling crash. If you feel you've got a reasonable hope of disabling the pursuer and injuring the occupants in the crash, you will be able to tolerate the loss of your transportation. Even if the occupants escape injury, they'll be on foot, too, with their vehicle disabled, and you may not be any worse off than on wheels.

The advantage of this technique is that you can do it alone. You don't need help in stopping and turning your car to block the road, and fleeing on foot without having to worry about a companion is easier.

Another point in favor of it comes when there are the inevitable complications with the police. Bullet holes are hard to explain away, but abandoning your vehicle because you fear for your life is plausible enough to avoid serious trouble, except from the insurance company.

Ditching one pursuer is much easier than evading several. If you feel there are other cars following you, the normal methods won't work, as one or more cars will be on a parallel street or farther behind, to defeat your evasive actions.

The only hope is to drive on an isolated road, and to block the road. This will dam them all up behind the block, which can be a disabled vehicle as noted above.

DECOYS, DISGUISE,
AND DECEPTION

"The police are never there when you need them."
The police role is reactive, arriving after the crime's
over, and the result is low clearance and conviction
rates.

The chances of arrest and conviction increase greatly
when the police catch the criminal in the act. One way
of doing this is by "pro-active" measures—undercover
and decoy operations.

Decoys are suitable targets laid in front of potential
criminals. They can be people or inanimate objects. An
expensive car parked on a side street at night can be a
decoy. Live decoys, police agents playing the role of
vulnerable targets, are the most interesting part of this
subject. The police use these in response to recent
crime patterns. If, for example, businessmen have been
robbed while making night deposits at banks, a police
agent playing this role is likely to attract such a crime,
giving the police the chance to apprehend the criminal
in the act.

In decoy operations, there's little need for elaborate
physical disguise, but role-playing is essential. There's
no need to resemble a particular individual, as
criminals are usually unacquainted with their victims.

It's important to match the decoy to the need.[1] If there's been a rash of taxi hold-ups, dressing decoys as nuns would be pointless.

Playing the role is the biggest problem. Police officers behave in certain ways, which will alert potential criminals if the decoy doesn't learn to change his behavior. A decoy who walks down the street alertly and confidently, looking into every doorway he passes, will give himself away. If he plays an elderly man, he'll have to learn to walk slowly and hesitantly, perhaps with a slight stoop, his eyes on the ground in front of him.

If the victims have been women, this poses a special problem. It's very difficult to disguise a two hundred pound officer as an eighty-year-old grandmother or a teenage schoolgirl. There have been much publicized efforts by police to disguise themselves as women, highlighted by the press for their entertainment value because the officers looked ridiculous in their high heels and short skirts over hairy legs.

It's better to use policewomen. Even a male with a slight build will have a hard time mimicking the way a woman moves and walks. Except for transvestites, who practice imitating women extensively, men usually can't play the role well.

Like her male counterpart, the decoy policewoman must play the role. She must not show alertness by scanning everyone as a possible threat.

The decoy must appear as a vulnerable target, by using role-playing and disguise. Not appearing physically fit and powerful is an art. Long sleeves and loose clothing will conceal bulging muscles. Choosing an officer who is small but wiry is another solution.

The physical disguise can be simple, depending on the situation. If muggers have been hitting insurance agents recently, it's only necessary to dress as most of the victims do, with a three-piece suit and a briefcase.

It's also important to avoid the giveaway physical signs of a police officer, such as a bulge on the hip.

Props can be more than a briefcase, such as a "Michigan Bankroll," a stack of one-dollar bills or paper cut to size with a few real, high-value bills on the outside,[2] or eyeglasses, with their connotation of vulnerability, to aid the illusion.

Attacks on derelicts, such as the "bum-burning" epidemics that occured in New York and Boston during the last two decades, call for equally simple disguises. Old, worn clothing and an unkempt, unshaven appearance will do. The prop can be a paper bag containing a wine bottle. Face make-up, a creme that gives a sallow complexion, will help. So will false whiskers, but it's easier to let the whiskers grow out naturally. Five days' growth is adequate, and there's no need to comb or shape the beard.

Physical bulk is only part of the effect. It aids the illusion of vulnerability to seem tired, not alert. Taking short steps and walking slowly with downcast eyes helps this illusion. Showing lack of coordination adds to this and can even suggest intoxication. Fumbling with or dropping a briefcase or keys, adds to an unsteady walk to simulate vulnerability.

Getting down on hands and knees to search for dropped objects is extreme, but it's convincing. This presents an extremely vulnerable state, and can precipitate an attack.

Carrying something that's an obvious burden enhances the illusion of vulnerability. Grocery bags look cumbersome, although they may be very light. A grocery bag can also conceal a gun. A cane or crutches also help. A wheelchair may be useful.

Physical disguise is not as important as acting the role. Face make-up does not produce victim-like behavior, but role-playing will.

The decoy must fit in with the locale.[3] He must not seem out of place.

Facing the danger of imminent attack requires self-control. It helps to have faith in the alertness and competence of the back-up officers.

The backups are really doing a sort of surveillance duty. They, too, must play roles, and fit in with the locale. They must have one additional quality, being inconspicuous or invisible. The decoy must be out in the open. The backups must fade into the background until the moment to act.

Sources

1. *Police Marksman*, March/April, 1980. p. 6.
2. *Ibid.*, May/June, 1982, p. 41.
3. *Ibid.*, March/April, 1980. p. 6.

PHYSICAL SEARCH

The phrase "bag job," covers entering premises for a physical search. The police can do this with a search warrant, or with the owner's consent, but a private citizen can't get a search warrant. Nevertheless, there are searches, although illegal. Watergate was an example of such a search.

There are different degrees of illegality.

Trespassing is the lowest grade of offense. Usually, this means going onto someone's property, but not into a building.

Breaking and entering is the next level. This means just that, entering by breaking in, but not necessarily stealing anything.

Burglary is the highest level. This may be simply B&E at night, as in some states, or it may involve stealing.

Penalties vary, depending on the jurisdiction, the judge, and other factors. The offense may be a misdemeanor or a felony.

The citizen has an advantage over the police in some situations. If, for example, you suspect your wife's loyalty is not all it could be, you can search her effects without fear of legal reprisal. You'll want to do it when she's not home, to avoid an argument.

Similarly, there are other areas open to you. Searching on the job is more a matter of doing it unseen than avoiding the law. You may suspect an employee of theft, in which case you can search his work station, and possibly his locker, without running afoul of the law. Searching his car is another problem, and generally you won't be able to do this legally.

If you're an employee, your situation is less solid. You don't own the premises, and this sharply limits your authority. If you suspect someone's trying to "frame" you, you'll have to take the risk of searching in full knowledge that you might, if caught, be letting yourself in for suspicion of more serious acts.

An advantage you may have as an employee, is the keys to the plant. This eliminates the problem of getting in. If you leave traces of the search, you may be on the suspect list because of these keys.

You may want to gain access to someone else's premises to get information. This puts you squarely on the wrong side of the law, and you risk arrest and prosecution if caught. The basic question you have to answer before starting to plan a search or a covert entry is whether you need evidence that will stand up in court. If you do, keep in mind that you'll not only have to present the evidence, but explain where and how you got it. This requirement rules out any illegal action.

You may, on the other hand, just need a "lead," something which will tell you where you can find, and obtain legally, information or evidence you can present in court. In such a case, you'll usually be able to keep your illegally obtained lead deeply buried.

Breaking In

If you have a compelling reason, you many want to take the risk. If so, the first step is to know the premises—the physical layout: doors, windows, locks, and alarm systems, if any. You must also know the schedule—the hours when the building is occupied. Professional criminals call this "casing the joint." This will help you judge whether or not you can do it, and what your chances of getting away with it are.

Once you choose the time and place, gaining access is the next step. There are roughly two ways of getting in: brute force and finesse.

Brute force means just smashing a door or window. This is practical in some areas, as there's nobody close enough to hear the noise at night. In others, any commotion will attract attention, and perhaps the police.

For a brute force entry, you'll need a few tools. A hammer, a crowbar, or perhaps as little as a rock, if you can gain access by breaking a window.

Before breaking anything, examine the area closely. Ideally, you should do this while "casing" your target. Fumbling in the dark is the worst way to do it. Knowing your mode of entry in advance will enable you to bring only the tools you'll need.

You might be able to release a window latch with a knife blade. A knife blade will also release a spring-bolt door latch. You might be able to get in a door by removing the hinge pins. Try to do the least damage, because this makes the least noise.

Breaking a window is a fairly straightforward way of gaining entry. In so doing, you can avoid the noise of shattering glass by putting masking tape on the window before you break it. Several sheets of wet newspaper will work as well.

Using finesse means lockpicking and circumventing any intrusion alarms. Picking the locks can be easy or hard, depending on your skill and the condition of the lock. Developing skill at lockpicking takes time and effort. There are some books on the subject,[1] but it takes practice to become proficient.

Alarms

One problem you may face is an alarm system. There are all sorts, from simple metal tapes on the windows to magnetic detectors, sonic alarms, induction detectors, and infra-red sensors. Some are easy to overcome, while others take a lot of specialized knowledge.

One huge advantage you have is that, if you do your homework, all the necessary information on alarm systems will be available to you openly. Manufacturers and distributors send product literature to anyone who wants it. This enables you, once you know what sort of intrusion detection device is in use, to get brochures in four colors on the devices. You'll know whether the system operates with wires or by radio. You'll learn if you can disable it by cutting the power supply, or whether it has a built-in battery as backup power.

Surprisingly, many alarms only flash lights and ring bells, not being connected to any central office. The result is that if there's nobody in the area to note the signals, the system will be ineffective. Also, it's a simple matter to cover a flashing light or to muffle the sound of a bell or gong.

To start doping out the alarm system, it's only necessary to look for the label on the main unit. It will have the manufacturer's name and the model number. Getting the literature can be as easy as looking in the yellow pages and, if there's a dealer in town, going to the showroom and examining the units. Posing as a possible buyer will get you answers to detailed questions, such as, "What protection does this have against cutting the wires?"

Generally, a manufacturer makes more than one piece of hardware. He has a "line," an assortment of modules to fit the needs of different customers. At the showroom, you can see what these modules look like, and learn what they do.[2]

One useful trick to lessen the effectiveness of a "silent alarm" is to trip it repeatedly if you can. Some of them are easy to trip from outside. If there's a sonic or seismic sensor, a heavy blow against an outside wall might be enough to set it off. If the system has metallic tape on the windows, cracking the glass lightly, just enough to break the tape, will set off the alarm. A magnetic sensor on a door or a window can be tripped by pounding on or shaking the door, if it's loose. Repeated false alarms will convince the central office that the system is malfunctioning, and any subsequent reaction will be slowed down.

Once you know what the alarm system on the premises does, and whether or not you'll be able to pick the locks, you can plan your entry. You have two choices:

(1) An entry by stealth, picking the lock and bypassing the alarm, if there is one.

(2) A "smash and grab," in which you know you're going to make noise and set off an alarm, and hope to escape before the police arrive.

If you do your homework properly, you'll know what you're facing before you go in. You'll avoid being surprised, and a surprise can be disastrous.

If you're going to have to make a quick entry and exit, you'll have to plan even more carefully. You'll need to plan your getaway, allowing yourself a margin of safety before anyone shows up. There won't be any time to waste, and you'll have to know what you're looking for. A detailed and leisurely search will be a luxury.

What you're seeking may be hidden. There are all sorts of clever, imaginative ways to hide things.[3] This can involve a long search, but you may not have the time. If you already know where what you want is located, it'll save you hours of searching.

The next decision involves disguising your intent. Covering the intent can be critical for you, as an entry aimed at the evidence you seek might narrow the suspect list to one person: yourself.

Unless the physical security is very poor, you may not be able to avoid leaving traces of your entry. You may have good reason for not wanting your target to know that someone's been seeking certain evidence, in which case you'll want to disguise the entry as a simple burglary. Taking valuables along with your real objective helps to mislead the owner of the premises. If there's a safe, leaving some tool marks around the door will suggest an attempt at burglary.

Knowing the personality of your target is always helpful. Some people don't take many precautions against burglary or search. Others are so concerned that they might be described as "paranoid," and they are constantly preoccupied with means of detecting a covert search. They may leave a match stick in the door jamb, to detect if their door's been opened in their absence, or leave objects arranged in a set pattern, to see if anything's been moved upon their return. These "James Bond" techniques are simple, and they work very well.

It's possible to enhance the effectiveness and speed of your search by some inexpensive technical means.

One good example is a metal detector, which detects both ferrous and nonferrous metals. This can help in locating a hidden strongbox, or a weapon.[4]

Postal Interception

In some instances, you may want to get a look at someone's mail. Doing this can be easy or hard, legal or illegal. If your target is a relative or employer, this might be very easy, as it's often possible to wander by and scan opened mail on a desk or table.

Without such "inside" access, an illegal method will be necessary. This is a serious crime, as even Postal Inspectors cannot open first-class mail without a court order, and diverting any mail from the addressee is illegal.

It can be done as simply as taking the mail from the mailbox after the mailman has dropped it in. This requires coming out in the open, with the risk of being seen.

There's a safer, "remote control" method, with less risk of detection. It involves engaging the services of a "mail drop,"[5] under an alias and paying cash, and sending in a change-of-address card on the target's mail. The mail will come to the mail drop, where it'll be easy to pick up. There's one serious problem with this method. It can't work for very long. After the first day or two, the target will notice that his mail deliveries have stopped, and when he inquires as to why, the Postal Inspector will get into it. Anyone using this method and trying to push his luck may find a Postal Inspector waiting for him when he goes to the mail drop on the third or fourth day.

We see from this that there are several legal and illegal methods of seeking evidence, and that their success depends on individual circumstances. There are definite risks to the illegal means, but at times it may seem worthwhile to take those risks.

Sources

1. *Locks, Picks, and Clicks,* Anonymous, Diamondback Press, Phoenix, AZ, 1975. This is one of many, and it covers forced entry from simple locks to safes. You can't learn lockpicking only from a book, and many hours of practice will be necessary before you develop some skill.

2. In one showroom which the author visited, some modules were installed and working, and it was possible to see their effectiveness. One infra-red detector, for example, would pick up human body heat in an arc that extended to seventy feet. This sort of direct experience is valuable for learning realistically what are the limits and possibilities of defeating or bypassing an alarm system. This manufacturer offered a central alarm unit, which when set off by a sensor, would send a tape recorded message to the police. This was an option which not every customer selected, and knowing what the hardware looks like helps greatly in assessing a system's capabilities.

3. *How To Hide Almost Anything,* David Krotz, New York, Macmillan Publishing Co., 1975, is aimed at hiding small valuables, including perhaps a drug "stash," and gives very explicit instructions on how to construct a variety of hiding places in a house or apartment. With the information gotten from such a book, and enough time, it's possible to *find* almost anything, no matter how cleverly the material is hidden.

4. Such a device is available from U.S. Ballistics and Armor Manufacturing Co., PO Box 24623, Tempe, AZ

85282, for twelve dollars, battery included. This device also detects electric currents, and signals by means of a red light-emitting diode, not a buzzer. This silent operation can be important in a covert action.

5. *Directory of Mail Drops in the United States and Canada*, Michael Hoy, Port Townsend, WA, Loompanics Unlimited, 1985.

STAKE OUTS:
OBSERVATION POSTS
AND FIXED SURVEILLANCE

The Hollywood or television version of a stake out is two men in a car parked some yards away from the subject premises, keeping it in sight through the windshield. In real life, two men in a car might as well hang out a sign saying "STAKE OUT" because they'd be that obvious. In some instances, a nervous resident might call the police.

Using an automobile as a fixed observation post is very amateurish, and is a method of last resort. So is standing in a doorway, although it may be useful when following a subject who goes into a building, and it becomes necessary to take up a position from which to observe the exits of the building and wait for him to come out.

The Hasty Stake Out

There must be a better way, and there is! A hasty stake out works much better if you can blend in with the other people in the area, and one way of doing so is to go into a nearby cafe, store, or restaurant. When you do this, the subject has to pick you out from a

78

crowd to "make" you, which is much harder than spotting a lone figure in a doorway.

Behavior is as important as physical surroundings. Your behavior must be appropriate to the situation. This is why standing in a doorway or sitting in a parked car are so conspicuous. People don't normally stand in doorways, unless it's raining or snowing, and they're waiting for a bus. People normally park their cars, lock them up, and leave. Anyone who sits in a car for more than a couple of minutes will stand out because he's not doing the normal thing.

One exception is a male-female team. They don't stand out if they sit in a car together. Anyone who sees them will interpret their behavior as that of lovers, especially if they're talking. At night, on a dark street, they can avoid seeming out of place by hugging and kissing. We can easily understand that in the same situation, a team of two men hugging and kissing would attract attention.

Setting up a hasty observation post is a matter of quick improvisation. Often, there are props available. A shoeshine stand or a stand-up lunch counter is often nearby in a city. A telephone booth is another prop. A gas station is yet another opportunity. This is of special value if the shadowing is likely to cover many miles, as it's wise to keep the gas tank as full as possible.

Behavior is as important as the prop. Normally, buying a tankful of gasoline doesn't take more than a couple of minutes. If it's necessary to stay in place longer, lifting the hood to check the oil, water, and battery is a way to stretch it out. Another way is to use the toilet, if there is more than one surveillant and they can take turns keeping the subject under observation. Toilet needs can become very important in a protracted surveillance, and taking advantage of the opportunity serves two purposes.

Going into a store, if nothing else is available, is another way of blending in and staying off the street. It's important to choose the appropriate store. A man would seem out of place in a cosmetics or lingerie shop, but not in a hardware or sporting goods store. A supermarket is "unisex" in this regard.

The ideal store is a self-service store, where you can linger and seem to study the merchandise without attracting attention. This is why a K-Mart or supermarket is the first choice. It's not hard to take up a position from which you can watch the street while seeming to be shopping. This also allows you to make a quick exit, without buying anything and getting tied up in a checkout line.

Bookstores are ideal for observation. The normal behavior is to browse, and some customers pore over books for hours without buying, and without even speaking with the clerk. If there's a bookstore with a large front window, this will be better than most other choices. Unfortunately, there aren't as many bookstores as there are supermarkets and bars.

A store without self-service is a second choice. In such a case, do a little window shopping first. Look for one that allows you to face the front of the store while talking with the clerk. Otherwise, you'll have to turn your head every few seconds, and this will attract attention. A little planning can avoid the need for clumsy improvisation later.

In the case of a bar, where it's customary to pay for drinks at the time the bartender pours them, there won't be any problem with getting out fast. Not all bars have windows that permit a view of the street, however, which impedes observation. If the stake out takes longer than a few minutes, alcohol consumption can cause a problem. Some people have the ability to "nurse" a beer for a long time, which is a definite advantage in such a situation.

Any place that sells food is worth a quick look. Selecting a table or place at the counter from which it's possible to observe the street is essential. Be prepared to pay quickly and get out. It's important to have enough money out in front of you to cover the check, because if you have to leave suddenly, forgetting to pay can cause a stir.

Using a phone booth for a few minutes' cover is more than just picking up the handset and pretending to talk. It helps to have a notebook open, and to pretend to be writing. A briefcase is a useful prop for this. If the phone booth is occupied, this is even better. Simply stand next to it, as if you're waiting to use the phone. This will enable you to look around and remain normal and inconspicuous.

A last resort, if nothing else is available, is to stop the car, lift the hood, and seem to be working under it. A stalled motorist won't usually arouse suspicion, but this improvised cover can't last for very long.

The Semi-Fixed Post

Sometimes it's possible to establish a somewhat more permanent position for a stake out. We've already seen that a car is one of the worst choices, but other motor vehicles can be much better. Any vehicle which doesn't permit easy observation of the inside will do, as long as it blends in with the locale.

The old TV cliche about a telephone company truck and two men in jumpsuits is so well-known that it doesn't work very well. In any event, it would be hard to justify two "telephone company" employees taking all day to check out the wiring at the top of the pole.

"City workers" digging up the street while observing a building is another Hollywood cliche that is hard to put into practice. The "city workers" would be embarrassed taking off and leaving a hole in the pavement if the subject they're observing suddenly decides to leave. Unless you're really a telephone company employee or a city worker, you'll have a hard time getting a suitable truck. If you decide to buy a similar truck, paint it to suit, and buy the auxiliary equipment, you'll probably attract attention from real telephone company employees, city workers, and certainly from the police if you try to dig up the street.

Vans and campers are very common, and they're almost ideal. If you own one, or can borrow one, you already have an advantage. If you must rent one, you'll be able to exploit it, although it will cost you some money.

It may be that your subject knows your vehicle. This gives you two choices: having it repainted or borrowing or renting another, to avoid his easily spotting you. Whether you need to do this or not also depends on how distinctive your vehicle is. If you have a plain blue van, in a locale where there are many vans and blue is a popular color, only the license plate will set you off. You can park far enough away so the plate is not easy to read, or is hidden by the vehicle in front of you.

The ideal set-up is one with curtains. Curtains permit looking out, but impede anyone's looking in. In using such a set-up, it's important to avoid being seen if you have to move the curtains to get a better view. It's also important not to be silhouetted, as when there are two windows on opposite sides of the van, and someone can see you moving between them. One way to avoid this is to block one off with a piece of cardboard behind the curtain, or tape a cardboard partition from the roof between the two windows if you need to observe from both sides.

The windshield will remain clear, of course, and a curtain or partition between the front seats and the back is essential, or anyone looking in the windshield will see you.

It's critical to remain back from the windows when observing, just as it is in a room. The interior of the van should be darker than the outside, to impede being seen. This is where curtains serve two functions, keeping excess light out and blocking direct view into the van. If the stake-out takes place overnight, it's important to be able to get out in darkness inside the vehicle, as the slightest glimmer of light will betray you.

The windows should be clean, not only for direct observation but to enable you to take photographs. When using a camera or binoculars, be sure to remain far enough inside to avoid direct sunlight on the lenses. A ray of sunlight can reflect very brightly, if the angle is right, and this can blow your cover.

If you have to take photographs, be sure to turn off the engine. The vibration will make it hard to get sharp exposures.

If you foresee a prolonged stake out, it helps to prepare for it in advance. You should provide for food and drink, and for toilet facilities. If your van isn't equipped as a camper, you'll have to improvise. In a pinch, some granola bars and a canteen of water will do for a short while. A milk carton can serve for urination, but if you need to stay in the van for twenty-four hours or longer, a portable camper's toilet will help a lot. You may not be able to leave the van for calls of nature, and being properly equipped will help.

If you have a camper, you can set up your stake out in style. Presumably, you'll have a refrigerator or icebox, a stove, and even toilet and shower facilities. This enables you, if you're properly stockpiled, to maintain the observation post for a week or more. A motor home, if one is available, is an absolute luxury.

Figure 6

A motor home parked in a block where its presence doesn't seem unusual gives all the comforts of home to the stake-out team. Its size and weight serve to mask movement inside, and to muffle the sound of voices somewhat. Curtains on the windows are normal, unlike a car, and serve to conceal signs of occupancy.

In such a case, the problems will be staying awake and avoiding any visible signs of occupancy. You'll have to be careful about noise, and be aware that moving around inside the vehicle may make it rock. If anyone passes by and notices movement or talking, it can give you away.

Parking can be a problem. First, the vehicle must "fit in," and appear normal in the area. A lavish motor home would seem out of place in a barrio, where the norm is junkers and stripped cars. A garish "hippie van" won't fit in a middle or upper-class neighborhood.

One point almost nobody considers is that the vehicle should not be of the make and year of the local police department's detective vehicles. Criminals are not the only ones aware of the unmarked cars that the police use, which are often plain four-door sedans of a popular make. Narcotics and undercover officers, aware of this, typically choose vehicles that are not at all like police cars, sometimes using vans, sports cars, and even luxury cars. If you own a vehicle that could be mistaken for an unmarked police car, use something else.

There may be local parking regulations that will impede your operation. If you have to park at a meter, you'll be forced to move the vehicle periodically. There may even be "No Parking" on the street.

A parking lot is the best choice, if one is within sight of the place you're observing. If it's a commercial lot, you'll have to pay a fee. If it's a shopping center parking lot, you'll be able to park free and go unnoticed if you park away from the entrances to the stores. Another advantage of a shopping center parking lot is that movement within the vehicle won't seem out of place, nor will entering and leaving. It's especially wise to choose a parking lot, even if some distance away, because the proper vehicle will enable you to use binoculars for observation, and the distance will aid in avoiding discovery.

Distance is important. People are likely to pay less attention to vehicles parked a block or two away than within a few yards of them. If the parking place is a logical one, such as a shopping center parking lot, the vehicle will remain psychologically invisible, although it may be quite large.

Another problem is leaving the vehicle. Normally, people park and leave their vehicles. A car or truck that parks on the street with the driver remaining inside is conspicuous. If the subject and/or his friends are watchful, and they see a vehicle pull in but nobody getting out, they'll pay close attention to it. This is where a two-man team is useful.

If your friend drives the vehicle, and gets out and walks away after he parks, this will seem normal, and you can remain concealed inside for the stake out. In such a case, it helps to have a portable CB, to enable you to call him back in a hurry if you have to move out.

Having a two or three man team for prolonged stake outs is essential. It's impossible to stay awake and alert around the clock, and observing in shifts is one solution.

An ideal set-up is a motor home in a shopping center parking lot. In some parts of the country, such a vehicle won't attract undue attention, even if parked overnight. If the vehicle is parked so that the door faces away from the subject premises, it will be possible to enter and leave it without being seen, blending in with other shoppers. The watchers can periodically get out to stretch their legs, shop for food, or even relieve each other if this is a large operation and they operate in shifts.

Good judgement will dictate the choice of food. It would be outlandish to try to barbecue steaks, but if in a shopping center it's easy to procure sandwiches, or even to take turns eating in a local restaurant.

The Fixed Stake Out

The basic prerequisite for a fixed observation post is to know the territory. If the stake-out is in your neighborhood, you'll have a head start in this regard. Knowing the layout is essential, because it enables you to choose the best observation post. Knowing the subject building, and all of its exits, enables you to cover it best. It may be necessary to set up more than one observation point, if you need to cover all sides of a building. Having help from a friend will enable you to do this. If you can't cover all the exits, you can cover the more likely ones.

You have to know every street, building, and alley. Knowing the surrounding area is important, because if your subject starts moving, you'll have to get moving yourself if you want to follow him. Knowing where you can pick him up after coming out of your stake out is vital or you'll lose him.

In certain instances, a fixed, or semi-permanent stake out is possible. This usually means a room in a building. If you own or rent the premises, you can easily set up a stake out. If you're a businessman concerned with employee theft, you can camp out in your office at night if you normally leave after the others, or let yourself in again after the others leave. The only problem might be that a dishonest employee might himself have your building staked out, and discover your effort.

If there's more than one entrance, you can make a big show of leaving at the normal time, then park your car a few blocks away and return through an alley and enter unseen through a back door.[1]

One good quality of an observation post is having an entrance not visible from the subject building, so you can't be seen entering and leaving your stake out position. If the entrance is visible, you'll have to minimize the chances of being seen by cutting down your trips.

If it's necessary to rent a room, you'll want to keep your reason secret from the landlord or rental agent, as he may talk, or even be a friend of your subject's. Unless you're a police officer, you won't be able to approach a stranger and ask for the use of his premises.

Another danger is having the landlord suspect that you're doing something illegal. You know that you're doing a surveillance, but he might perceive it differently, and conclude that you're a narcotics trafficker. In such a case, you might come under surveillance from the police, or even have to face questioning.

Probably the greatest danger is if your surveillance is connected with something illegal. If you're also wiretapping, you'll naturally be very careful while installing the tap, but you might relax your caution while doing the legal part. Any attention which brings investigation of your activities can lead to the illegal part. This is why you should be vigilant throughout.

You will have to move in some equipment, even for the most austere stake out. Some of the items can be:

● Food.

● Drink.

● Camera.

● Binoculars or telescope.

● Electronic equipment.

While the sight of a man carrying a cooler or cardboard box doesn't attract undue attention, a pair of binoculars might. Keep any optical or other specialized equipment in a box or bag, to avoid disclosing your purpose.

Avoiding detection while in the observation post is essential. One of the first things you should do when you get in is to draw all the blinds, curtains and drapes almost shut, and to turn out any lights. Set up your post so you can see your target from back in the room. A giveaway is to put your face close to the window, or to draw back drapes to get a better view. Select your field of view, and leave it that way! Bring a small flashlight with you for use at night. Turning on the room lights in a residential neighborhood can seem normal, because people often do get up during the night, but in a commercial area it will be a giveaway!

Another, but less important problem is noise. It's unnecessary to keep total silence. This will depend on the location of the observation post. One in an attic which is normally unoccupied will require silence if there are people on the floor below who might hear voices or footsteps. Using an office will permit normal office noises during normal business hours, and using an apartment or furnished room gives an even greater block of time during which you can allow the normal noises of occupancy.

There's a special problem connected with renting stake outs. The hours of apparent occupancy must seem normal. An apartment in which two men sit all day will attract attention. So will an office which is occupied twenty-four hours a day. This is where a male and female stake out team is useful. It's not unusual for the "husband" to go to work in the morning, leaving the "wife" home. With an office or other business premises, there can be "normal" activity during business hours, but it will help if neighbors see someone lock up and leave at normal closing time.

If there's electronic surveillance, headphones are essential. The noise of a loudspeaker will be conspicuous at night.

A last resort is a rooftop or outdoor observation post. Any rooftop post leaves you vulnerable, because it's hard to avoid being silhoutted against the sky when making an observation. An outdoor post will do, if it's possible to make an improvisation that lets you fit in with the neighborhood. If there's a nearby tennis court, and a line of people waiting to play, you can join the end of the line if you're properly dressed.

Rural Observation Posts

Wide open spaces give you more freedom, but they also expose you more to observation, by your subject or others. When selecting an observation post, you may choose a gully, rock formation, or shrubbery. An important point is that you should choose a spot that gives you all-round cover. Someone else might come along, see you before you can hide, and blow your cover.

Rural people usually know their neighbors, and spot immediately anyone who doesn't "belong." Thick woods usually give good all-round cover. It may be necessary to approach the post at night, to reduce the chances of meeting someone. This means that warm clothing is necessary, and as the observation's likely to be until the next evening, food and drink.

Finding a place to leave a vehicle can be a serious problem. If there are no state campgrounds nearby, it might be necessary to have a friend drive you to a point near your cover and drop you off.

It would be going too far to wear camouflage clothing and camo colors on your face, as meeting someone would certainly arouse suspicion. Dark clothing is helpful, and removing or covering anything shiny, such as a belt buckle, will help you stay unseen.

Noise carries far on a quiet night, and leaving behind coins and other objects that can rattle and betray you is a good step. Choice of clothing material is important too, because some fabrics, such as nylon, are noisy when rubbing against brush. Dacron or cotton, and even wool, are far better.

In an extreme situation, you may be obliged to dig a foxhole, and cover it with branches. If this becomes necessary, do your digging at night, and have all loose soil and other evidence of digging covered up or scattered by first light.

The Edge of The Sword

Some situations suggest an armed stake out. If you're a shopkeeper in an area that has had a wave of robberies, or if you work in a gas station or pharmacy, both of which are favorite targets for stick-up artists, you may be tempted to prepare yourself for a robbery, and plan to resist it.

There are good reasons for doing this. The police can't protect you. Usually, they arrive only after the crime is over, to interview the victims and write their reports. Their rate of clearance of robberies is nowhere near 100%, and they certainly won't put a policeman in front of your door to protect you. Occasionally, some departments have "stake out squads," or "street crime units," groups of specialists who stake out possible targets in high-risk areas, but this is rare.

The basic fact is that the armed citizen is the first line of defense against crime. He's the cutting edge of the sword, and the police, in reality, are only backups. When they arrive, they depend on the citizen to provide descriptions, identify the suspects, and later testify in court. Throughout, even if the criminal is caught and convicted, the citizen is the central figure in the process.

In most states, it's legal to use deadly force in self-defense. In most states, it's legal to own a firearm, and to carry it while on one's own property, even if concealed. This gives the opportunity to set up an armed defense against the prospect of a robbery. Having the opportunity is one thing—planning a competent defense is another.

Carrying a gun is not enough. Knowing how and when to use it is essential. Using proper tactics is critical. There are several steps required before you can consider yourself competent, and ignoring them can bring you trouble.

First, select a handgun and learn to use it. You may need instruction at a "shooting school," or you may take naturally to the low grade of marksmanship required and learn on your own. Whatever the case, you must be able to hit a man-size target at close range, no greater than the longest dimension of your business. You must be able to hit consistently, without missing, because a wild shot can endanger innocent people and expose you to a lawsuit. This is why many high-risk targets, such as banks, don't arm their employees or even have armed guards any more. They know that a lawsuit can cost them far more than the amount of money a robber may take.

It is important to know the law in your locale, so you'll have some legal guidelines for action. Some defenders have opened fire in situations they considered self-defense, only to find out when the police arrived that they were the guilty parties, and liable to civil and criminal prosecution. If you're a businessman, you probably have a lawyer. Otherwise, a good source of free information is the county attorney. A member of his staff will probably be willing to discuss the law as it relates to self-defense and deadly force.

You must protect yourself physically, too. This means planning spots in your store where you can jump for cover from any bullets fired at you. Reinforcing the back of a counter with a sheet of half-inch steel will stop any pistol bullet, and most rifle shots.

Wearing body armor will help a lot. Generally, soft body armor that's light and comfortable enough to wear all day will not cover the whole body, nor even the entire torso, but will cover the vital areas in the torso. There are three problems with body armor:

(1) Many body armor manufacturers won't sell it to civilians, stating self-righteously that they sell only to police to avoid its falling into the hands of criminals. This is like the gun control argument, ignoring the fact that many civilians have legitimate uses for body armor, and that many more civilians are feloniously killed than police officers. At least one body armor manufacturer recognizes the need of civilians for body armor, and will sell to them.[2]

(2) Body armor gives only partial protection. It's not a "bullet-proof" vest, won't stop all bullets, and doesn't protect every vulnerable area of the body, such as the head. This is why it's important not to be overconfident, and to make good use of cover and tactics.

(3) Some body armor is too heavy or too uncomfortable to wear all day. There are many body armor manufacturers with many different designs, and some of them are atrocious, as well as expensive. A vest that gives a very high level of protection, but is too

heavy or bulky to wear, is worse than a lighter one that you can wear all day. Partial protection all the time is better than perfect protection none of the time.

Tactics are all-important. You should plan, and rehearse, what you will do in case of a robbery. Running through a dummy exercise will show up the weak points in your plan, and point out instances in which it's better to do nothing.

Plan how you'll get to your covered firing position. A good place for this is next to the cash register, as this is a likely area for you to be if the robber tells you to hand over your money. You should also plan for another position, in case the robber orders you to move clear of the register while he removes the money himself.

If you have employees, they should be part of the plan. If they want to carry a handgun, set up firing positions for them. If not, tell them where to duck when the action starts. They should also, if you plan armed resistance, have the choice of wearing body armor.

Customers pose a special problem. You don't want to hit innocent people in the cross-fire, and having customers in the store is one of the cases in which you might decide it's better to hand over the money than to risk a shootout. Fortunately, robbers usually strike when there are no other people on the premises, because it gives them fewer people to watch, and they're usually aware of the possibility that one of the customers may be an off-duty cop.

A backroom stake out is the best, but it consumes manpower. It involves staying in a back room, with an open doorway or a two-way mirror giving a view of the store, and being prepared to intervene with a heavy weapon. Having a shotgun is practical when it's not necessary to conceal it.

A shotgun is a good choice.[3] It's powerful enough for the job, and buckshot doesn't carry as far as a rifle or pistol bullet, which is very important in a built-up area. Considering the short range involved, light buckshot, such as #4, is a good choice. The lighter pellets will give a dense pattern at short range, and will lose velocity faster than heavier ones, such as #00. If the range is very short, thirty feet or less, #8 birdshot is better. Even with a cylindrical, (unchoked) barrel it will produce a very dense pattern at ranges up to twenty feet, yet will scatter enough beyond thirty feet so the charge will not go through both sides of an interior wall. This is important, as you want to restrict the firepower to avoid endangering innocent people.

Figure 7 is a diagram of a typical business, and shows one plan of armed defense that might apply. The cash register, A, has a sheet of steel built into the counter below it. The two employees, B and C, have pre-assigned stations where they can go if a gunfight erupts. Again, there's 1/2 inch sheet steel built into the counters where they are. D is the customer area, with a couple of product displays in the middle of the floor.

An essential point is that these displays should not offer any cover to a gunman. Stacks of cans are out of the question, as they'll stop many bullets. Cereal boxes are better, as part of the plan is to provide maximum protection for yourself and your employees and deny it to a gunman.

Assuming the employees will take active roles in defense, their locations become critical. Note that they can engage a gunman with cross-fire wherever he might be in the customer area. There's no place to hide that will keep him out of sight of all of the store personnel.

In laying out cross-fire, it's important for the defenders to avoid firing toward each other. Planning this in advance will avoid accidental injuries.

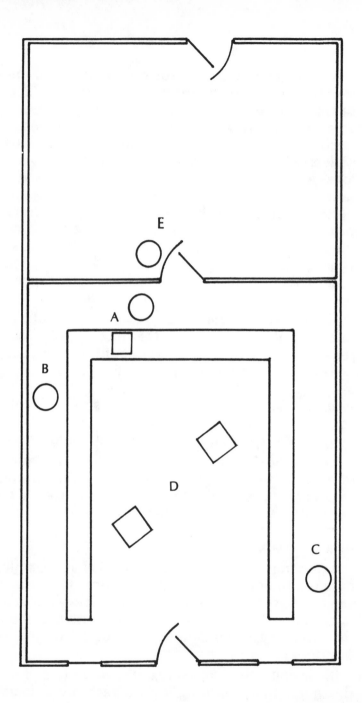

Figure 7

The back room, E, gives yet another prospect for the businessman in a high-risk area. Armed with a shotgun, he can observe the store through the partly opened door, revealing himself only when a robbery occurs. The drawback is that standing guard this way prevents him from taking care of business up front.

The advantage is that this simplifies the plan. He can emerge at the right moment, taking the gunman by surprise, without requiring the employees to be armed. This is an important point. Not everyone longs to be a gunfighter, and not everyone is familiar with weapons. Some people are even afraid of weapons. If some of the employees don't want to be armed, their task is simply to take cover.

Ideally, of course, the stickup artist should have to face gunfire from several directions at once, but it doesn't always work out this well. Whatever the case, there should be a clear plan before the action starts.

In this regard, it's important to note that in many states, a robber who shows a weapon in effect gives the defender a license to kill. With this in mind, the best plan is to open fire and keep shooting until the gunman goes down. This reduces the chances of his firing back, and perhaps hitting one of the defenders or an innocent person with a ricochet.

There's no moral obligation to shoot to wound only. If the gunman lives, there'll be a trial, which means taking time off from work to testify. If the shootout is fatal to the gunman, there will be no need for a trial.

Frustrations

Finding the time to carry out a surveillance is hard enough for someone who has to hold a job, but the possibly missed opportunities while your post is unmanned can spoil your whole effort. Unfortunately, this is what comes with the territory. Even the police, with their manpower and other resources, don't score 100%, and you should be prepared for failure. The fact is that you're more likely to fail than to succeed, and you need the emotional stamina to cope with this.

As a start, you should expect to spend many nonproductive hours in surveillance, as significant events aren't likely to happen to suit your schedule. A lot depends on how far you're prepared to go, and how important to you results are. If your reason is critically important, you'll have the motivation to spend some sleepless nights, or even take time off from work and accept the loss in pay involved.

You may spend a lot of money if you're well-motivated, and the prospect of seeing it wasted because nothing turned up can be discouraging. This is a very real risk, and you should understand this before you start.

If you're alone in your effort, it will be harder. The emotional support that members of a team give each other is significant, and without this you'll need a lot of determination to carry you through.

Sources

1. In one instance, this is exactly what happened. A business had been plagued by an epidemic of sabotage, possibly by a disgruntled employee. The foreman enlisted the aid of two loyal employees and staked out the place, using several different methods.

For several weeks, the three would leave at the normal time, pick up some sandwiches and thermos bottles of coffee, and return after dark, parking their cars in a shopping center parking lot across the street.

They'd leave their cars, and go through the back streets to enter by the alley door, which the foreman had left unlocked and unbolted. Keeping well away from the windows, they would make themselves comfortable and wait for something to happen. In some ways, they were sloppy. They smoked while sitting at desks that were visible from the street, which might have given them away to anyone passing by. Bored, they chit-chatted, although in low voices.

Suspecting they might have been seen entering the building, or perhaps leaving it after a stake out, they changed their tactics. Instead, they returned after dark to the shopping center across the street, parking behind a row of cars and keeping the building under observation with binoculars. Again, nothing happened.

This shows some of the uncertainties of a stake out. The guilty party, if a fellow employee, might have driven by and recognized one of the cars. They might have been seen by chance entering the building surreptitiously. It only takes one mistake to give the game away. One of the suspects happened to live across the street. If indeed he was guilty, his house gave him a perfect place for observation to detect a stake out.

Another problem was that there were a couple of false alarms while they were staking out the premises from across the road. In one case, a drunk fumbling at the back door brought the watchers screeching up in their cars, headlights on and piling out to apprehend the "suspect." This very visible action would have given it away to anyone watching.

2. Silent Partner, Inc., 612-18 Third Street, Gretna, LA 70053. Toll-free # 1-800-321-5741. Their lightest model weighs 1.3 pounds with armor insert, is made like a mesh T-shirt, and is comfortable enough to wear all

day. It takes soft armor inserts, the lightest of which will stop .38 Special, and will accept heavier inserts to stop heavier calibers. The prices start at about $125.00 for a vest and armor insert. Silent Partner makes both male and female models.

3. *The Shotgun in Combat*, Tony Lesce, Paladin Press 1985.

PHOTOGRAPHIC
SURVEILLANCE

Let's start by defining photographic surveillance: *Photographic surveillance is photographing the subject without his awareness.* This leaves out a lot of unnecessary material, such as passport photos, and police mug shots. It excludes cameras in banks and shops, placed openly to record holdups.

There are several reasons why you might need photographs of your subject:

(1) As evidence. If, for example, you're the owner of a business, and you know someone is stealing from you, photographs might serve as evidence for a prosecution. Unless you're prepared to make an arrest on the spot, you'll prefer to take the photographs covertly. This excludes flash photography.

(2) For future reference and comparison. You might want a record of the cars parked in a certain place, or you might need a photograph of a subject to show to another person, for possible identification. For both cases, you'll probably prefer that the subject not know you're photographing him.

The Environment

You may have to take pictures in broad daylight, or the light might be dim. You'll have to adapt your techniques to the situation.

You may be able to get close, photographing your subject from across a room or street, or the range may be great. Again, you'll have to tailor your methods to the needs.

You may be able to take the pictures yourself, or you may have to have an automatic camera, tripped by a remote release. This can come about when you need to cover an area for a long period of time, as in the case of thefts from a store, and can't man the post for 24 hours a day. In such a case, you'll have to jury-rig a device to trip the shutter when someone opens the door or window, or devise another expedient.

Equipment

This is a nuts-and-bolts book, and this discussion of equipment will be a short, no-nonsense one, with specific recommendations drawn from the author's experience. Any discussion of equipment is likely to offend someone who doesn't find his favorite hardware included, or who disagrees with the choices. Unfortunately, there's no easy way to resolve such conflicts. Different people have different needs, and will prefer different equipment. There's also more photographic equipment on the market than it's possible to cover in a short chapter, and so most will remain uncovered.

If you have a favorite camera, and it works well for you, by all means try to work with it before buying anything else.

Cameras

The 35mm camera is here to stay, for several reasons, some of which make it a good choice for surveillance:

(1) It's light and compact, compared to larger format cameras.

(2) It's commonly available, and takes commonly available film of many types.

(3) It gives negatives of excellent quality, enough to make 16 x 20 prints and larger, assuming the right film and competent use.

(4) It accepts a variety of accessories, such as telephoto lenses, and remote releases.

(5) Most 35mm single-lens reflex cameras have behind-the-lens metering, which is important when using different lenses of different efficiency, and for getting a reading without getting close to the subject.

(6) The price is right. It's possible to buy a 35mm camera of excellent quality for under $200. Larger format cameras cost a lot more, and the accessories are much more expensive.

Price is important. The CIA and other government agencies can afford exotic and expensive equipment, but usually the private citizen has to work on a budget, and a discussion of equipment that's priced out of sight isn't helpful. Fortunately, modestly-priced equipment is also very good quality equipment, and top-notch cameras are available in the $200 bracket, although the purists and snobs who own Leicas and Nikons will turn up their noses.

One aspect of price which none of the photography experts discuss is that it's as easy to drop or lose an expensive camera as it is a cheap one. Accidents happen. As this isn't a photography magazine, and does not contain advertisements for cameras, the author doesn't care if he offends the manufacturer of high-priced equipment by pointing this out. An expensive camera will cost you more to repair or replace. Think about this carefully.

More important than the equipment is knowing how to use it. This set of skills is impossible to learn from reading one chapter. It's necessary to learn more, and to practice. There are many good books available in libraries, and Kodak publishes a number of practical guides on photography.

The author's favorite brand is Olympus. These cameras, whether the relatively simple OM-1, or the more sophisticated OM-G, are very well made, with sharp lenses and smooth shutter and mirror mechanisms. The behind-the-lens metering and bayonet-mount lenses make changing easy, and there's a variety of lenses available at different prices.

This is not to say that other brands aren't as good. Many are. Minolta, Canon, and Pentax are some other brands with good reputations because they work well for other people.

Lens quality is not as important as the advertisements claim. Excellent resolution (sharpness) on the optical test bench doesn't necessarily mean that a super-sharp image will record on the film. There are several problems which can degrade sharpness, no matter how good the lens:

(1) Camera vibration. This can came about through a rough mirror and shutter mechanism, or through camera shake, caused by using too low a shutter speed for the conditions.

(2) Improper use. This can come from choosing the wrong film, or improper bracing of the camera when using low shutter speeds, or just clumsy handling. This can also come about through overexposure and overdevelopment, which increases grain and burns out fine detail.

(3) Film limitations. Most 35mm lenses made today can resolve about 300 lines per millimeter. Unfortunately, even the best films can't do that. We'll look at films later.

Lenses

What lens do you need? That depends on the situation. A "normal" 50mm lens is fine for most purposes, but if you have to set up a stake-out at a distance, you may need a telephoto lens. Roughly, the more power (magnification), the higher the cost.

If you're not sure of how much magnification you'll need or if you need to photograph in different situations, a zoom lens is a good investment. One zoom lens replaces a number of different fixed-focal length ones. It's cheaper to buy one zoom lens, and easier to carry only one lens than an assortment of telephotos.

While it's true that zoom lenses aren't as sharp as fixed lenses, in practice this doesn't matter. The good modern zooms, costing between two and three hundred dollars, are more than adequate for the task, mainly because of camera and film limitations, which prevent getting the full benefit from a super-sharp lens.

It's harder to hold a zoom or telephoto lens steady. This is because the lens magnifies not only the subject, but camera movement. You'll have to experiment to find the shutter speed you need for best sharpness in the conditions you'll be facing.

A good, all-round zoom lens for the Olympus is the Vivitar Auto-Zoom, F4.5 75-260mm. It's not too heavy, is very sharp, and is rugged and easy to use. Its built-in lens hood is convenient when shooting against bright light, and it's mechanically reliable.

There are special purpose telescopes which will adapt to cameras, such as the Celestron. Usually, these are heavy bulky affairs, and are very expensive. While they permit photographing the license plate of a car at a distance of several miles, this is a rare requirement. A special problem associated with such extreme lenses is atmospheric turbulence. "Heat waves" usually spoil a photograph, because the high magnification also amplifies the effect of heat waves. A tripod or other solid mount is a must with these lenses. Some of the larger lenses need two tripods, or a combination of tripod and special brace.

Films

There are many types of film, and many brands. For brevity, it's necessary to limit the discussion to Kodak films. As with cameras, there are other good brands, and some which the author can recommend with a clear conscience are Agfa-Gevaert, Ilford, GAF, and Fuji. The author prefers Kodak because these films are commonly available, and have good latitude, which means that they forgive minor mistakes.

Depending on exposure and processing, this is a rough guide to film resolving power:
- Kodak Tri-X: 70 lines per millimeter.
- Kodak Plus-X: 90 lines.
- Kodak Panatomic-X: 110 lines.

How do these figures translate into practical sharpness? Let's look at the maximum enlargement size possible. Assuming proper exposure and development, adequate darkroom skills, and a good enlarger, we can get the following full-frame enlargements consistently:

- Tri-X: 8x10 enlargements.
- Plus-X: 11x14.
- Panatomic-X: 16x20.

Why would anyone want a print that measures 16x20 inches? Actually, 8x10 is a good practical size, but often it's necessary to blow the negative up further, cropping out some of the background, to get a good sized, clear print of the subject. This is when film resolution and good technique pay off. It might be necessary to blow up a photo of a car enough to read the license plate, or a house to read the address. It might be necessary to see what someone is holding in his hand. It might happen that it was impossible to approach the subject enough to fill the frame, making a blow-up necessary.

In some instances, where an extreme blow-up is necessary, it might be helpful to use a special film, such as Ilford Pan-F or Agfa Isopan F. The problem comes because these films are both very slow (exposure index between 10 and 25) and have little latitude. In other words, they're temperamental, and careful exposure and processing are necessary for best results. For large blow-ups, Panatomic-X will do most of the time, without the problem that the special films bring with them.

Sending film off for processing isn't practical, unless you're willing to settle for mediocre results, or willing to pay the price for custom processing. Doing it yourself, if you're careful, will give you better results at lower cost.

One exception is color film. Kodachrome, the sharpest of the bunch, is not designed for user-processing. The various Ektachromes, with moderate to very high speeds, are designed for home processing, but the chemicals don't have good storage life, and unless you plan to process half a dozen rolls at once, it'll be too costly.

Regarding color films for home processing, it's been the author's experience that the GAF color films are easier to use and process, as the system has more latitude, forgiving mistakes more than other brands.

Another reason for home processing is that it's possible to "push" film by extended development, to get higher sensitivity for dim-light photography.

One additional reason for home processing, black and white or color, is secrecy. This might be important to you, especially if the photographs have a sexual content.

Processing

Every camera hobbyist or professional has his favorite film and developer combination. For what they're worth, the author's choices are Kodak Plus-X and Edwal FG-7. These are the reasons:

(1) This is a good, all-round combination, enough to give an 11x14 enlargement.

(2) Plus-X is sensitive enough to permit using in a bus station, store, manufacturing plant, or sports arena with an exposure of approximately 1/30th sec. at F4.

(3) This combination has latitude, to compensate for minor mistakes, and is easy to use.

Other people prefer other developers, such as Kodak D-76 or Ethol UFG, both of which are excellent, and both of which the author has used extensively at times.

"Pushing" film has its limits. There's an increase in contrast and grain, the tiny silver crystals that make up the image. These both degrade sharpness. Usually, doubling the development time will increase the effective speed of the film by four, depending on the film-developer combination. Pushing is also possible with Ektachrome and the GAF color films, although the technique is more complex.

There's a common fallacy that a "super" developer will enable great speed from normal films. For the most part, this is untrue. It is true that some developers will give slightly more speed, about half a stop, but any more gain is at the expense of excessive grain and contrast. It's more practical, if you need more film speed, to choose the next faster film.

Legal Aspects

This may not matter for most purposes, but there can be legal problems in some instances. State laws vary; but some general guidelines follow.

It's legal to photograph anyone in a public place, but not on private property unless you own the property. This means that shooting someone through the window of his dwelling isn't legal. If you have to enter without the owner's permission, that is breaking and entering, or burglary, depending on how the law reads in your state.

It may be legal to photograph someone on private property if it's outdoors, and normally visible from the street or an alley. If it's necessary to climb a fence or otherwise penetrate a barrier, there may be a problem.

Under most conditions, you won't have to worry about the legalities of the photos you take. Most of them simply won't apply to you. You won't be concerned with model releases, giving permission for publication of the photographs, or copyright problems. What will concern you is avoiding violation of the criminal code, or getting caught at it.

If you plan to use the photographs in court, however, you must be careful to obtain them legally. The "exclusionary rule" supported both by state laws and court decisions, obliges a judge to throw out any evidence that's "tainted," that is, illegally obtained. If you think you'll need photos for evidence, check with your lawyer first.

Setting up the Stake Out

Finding a place from which to take photographs can be easy or difficult, depending on the situation. If you own the premises, or you're taking photos in daylight, it's easier than if you have to shoot at night or on someone else's property. The advantages of owning the property are that you can set up the camera almost anywhere you wish, and take exposure readings at your leisure, even shooting a test roll to check out your system.

A place of concealment can be very similar to that needed for a visual stake out. Generally, if you can see, you can take pictures. You'll have to hide yourself, yet leave an opening for the camera lens. Common sense is a good guide to finding a hiding place.

Take care when shooting through glass, whether it be a one-way mirror or a window. The best lens in the world won't help if the glass is dirty. You have to observe the same precautions as for visual observation, such as keeping the room lights low, and standing well back from the window to avoid being seen.

You may want to use a tripod, if time and space permit, and if the light is too low for a fast shutter speed. Lacking a tripod, bracing the camera solidly against a firm object will allow sharp photographs at low shutter speeds in many cases.

If a hasty set-up is needed, it's possible to steady the camera with an improvisation: Take a 1/4-20 bolt, and attach a six-foot long string to it. Screw the bolt into the tripod socket on the camera, and let the string dangle. When ready to shoot, step on the string, and pull up hard on the camera. This will give more steadiness than hand-holding, and it's cheap and light.

If you're using a telephoto lens in dim light, you're up against it. Telephoto lenses usually have smaller maximum F-stops than normal lenses, and this requires a slower shutter speed. As a telephoto lens usually requires a high shutter speed for sharpness, because the magnification increases the effect of camera vibration, your choice often is between a faster film which is less sharp, or using a tripod or brace, permitting a lower shutter speed.

Photographing from a Vehicle

This is necessary in some situations. One is using a vehicle for surveillance, and taking pictures of everyone approaching the suspect premises. In such a case, using a camera surreptitiously can be a problem. Bringing the camera up to make the exposure can attract attention.

One solution is to photograph from far away, using a telephoto lens. Another is to use a vehicle which permits movement inside without attracting attention. A van or motor home with curtained windows will do the trick. Make sure the windows are clean.

In some instances, it's necesary to take a "grab shot" rolling up near the suspect and shooting him by snapping the camera up quickly to take the shot, then down again before he can see it. In such a case, don't let the camera touch any part of the vehicle when making the exposure, as the vibration of the engine, transmitted through the body, will induce camera vibration and lose sharpness.

Sometimes it's necessary to take a photograph of a building for reference, such as planning a raid or surreptitious entry. In such a case, it helps to know the exact number and location of doors, windows, and other details which need careful study.[1]

The technique of "fly-by" photography isn't well-known, and is worth setting out here, because it's simple and financially within reach of most people. It requires a medium-speed film, such as Plus-X, and a motor drive. The need comes when it's necessary to record a building's many physical details, for planning a raid or other action. A fly-by is less conspicuous than parking down the street with a sketch pad, and making drawings and taking notes.

Depending on the camera, and whether bought new or used, a motor drive costs between fifty and three hundred dollars. The rate at which it fires varies from one per second to three per second.

The technique is to use the maximum shutter speed, usually 1/1000th of a second, and to drive by slowly, holding the camera up and shooting through the open window, without careful aiming and holding the camera only high enough to clear the car door. Taking a burst of exposures will usually yield several good ones with one pass. Of course, it's necessary to choose a moment when nobody is on the street, or observing the street, to avoid warning the subject that there's any unusual activity.

A fly-by requires daylight for success. This normally fits in with the needs of the situation. Plus-X film will allow an exposure of 1/1000th of a second at F 5.6 or F 8, enough to freeze the movement and allow enough depth of field.

Dim Light Photography

There are special techniques to enable you to take pictures in low-light that normally would be insufficient to permit photographs. One is using a very high speed film, such as Kodak 2475 Recording Film. With 8 minutes in Kodak DK-50, this film will permit an exposure index (ASA) of 4000. It's very grainy, however, and this will limit the size of the enlargements possible.

Lower on the scale, Tri-X will yield an exposure index of 1250 if processed for 11 minutes in D-76. Several other developers, such as Ethol UFG and Baumann Acufine will give even better results, the same speed with somewhat less grain and contrast.

Tri-X at normal speed, (400), processed in D-76 or UFG will give a good compromise between quality and speed.

One technique that will help is to "bracket," to make another exposure one stop over and another one stop under the correct one as indicated by the meter. This will increase the chances of getting a usable negative.

Determining the exposure when you can't show yourself can be a problem. With a behind-the-lens meter, part of the solution is in your hand. Unfortunately, many situations won't permit accurate use of such a meter, as when the subject is strongly illuminated under a street light and the background is dark.

One way of getting around this is to point the meter towards the light source, and give about two stops more exposure. This works because the subject, on the average, reflects about 18 or 20% of the light falling on him. The limitation is that you have to be the same distance from the light source as the subject, to get a fairly accurate reading.

Infra-Red Photography

Infra-red light is invisible to the human eye, but there are special films made to use it. This permits photography with supplementary illumination without the subject's becoming aware of it. Unfortunately, there are some problems, which is why infra-red photography is not in widespread use.

The first is that the light source, an infra-red bulb or an ordinary one with an infra-red filter over it, sometimes is visible. No filter is 100% efficient, and most leak a small amount of unwanted light. An infra-red bulb or filter will show up as a dull red glow if the subject looks directly at it.

The filter required is a Kodak Wratten #87[2] over the light source. This will illuminate the subject without creating a dazzling flash. It's still visible, however.

Another problem comes from the need to load and unload the camera in total darkness, because the film cassette doesn't block infra-red.[3] Special precautions during the processing are also necessary.

Yet another problem is that infra-red light does not come to the same point of focus as visible light, and it's necessary to change the setting on the camera. This can be done by calculation or by using the reference mark if the focusing ring has one. Because dim light photography normally requires a fairly wide F-stop, which gives shallow depth-of-field, there's not much room for error.

Summing up, it's clear that using conventional film is usually more practical. Using a faster film or a slower shutter speed will give more reliable and consistent results.

Electronic Scopes

"Starlight" scopes, first made famous by use in Vietnam, have their advantages and some severe limitations. They permit both viewing and photographing in extremely low light levels, electronically amplifying the existing light.[4]

The first problem is that they are very costly. Even a second-hand scope of Vietnam vintage, in good condition, will cost over $3,000. A modern scope, with second-generation electronics, can easily cost twice that.

The next problem is quality of the image. While it's true that you can see an image in very poor illumination, it often happens that the image isn't clear enough to be useful. When you look into one of these scopes, what you see is a green image, lacking in contrast. You see light, but sometimes objects will be invisible because they blend in with the background. This is the part the manufacturers don't tell you. In one test, a target with a colored figure appeared simply as a light rectangle.[5] In another test, a person standing in an alley only twenty yards away, without trying to conceal himself, blended in so well with the background that he was invisible through the scope.

Electronic scopes are bulky, usually about a foot long, and weigh from four to seven pounds. This makes them hard to conceal for surreptitious use, and the only hope is that the light will be too dim for the suspect to see them.

Remote-Control Photography

In order to leave the camera unattended, for surveillance over a long period of time, some sort of remote control is necessary. One way to do it is to have an electric switch trip a motor drive, if adaptable. Let's lay out one problem, and one possible solution.

You own a warehouse, and suspect that an employee has been letting himself in at night and stealing material. There's one door usually used for access to the loading dock. You mount a motor drive on an Olympus camera, and fit a remote control unit. This is a switch with a long wire and a jack which plugs into the motor drive, and is available from Radio Shack for about three dollars. You have to jury-rig a switch so that opening the door closes the circuit, firing the camera. There's enough light in your warehouse to permit using conventional film.

One possible problem is camera noise. This varies from one camera to another. Some click off quietly, while others have so much mirror slap that it sounds like a door slamming. You'll have to judge for yourself whether or not the camera noise will blend in with background noise.

Testing the System

This is essential, especially if using unfamiliar equipment or a new film. Often, there are unpleasant surprises, and it seems to be the rule that the more exotic and expensive the equipment, the more chance of a problem arising. Set up to shoot in a situation similar to the one you'll be facing when photographing your subject, and shoot and process a roll of film. Checking the results will give you warning of any problems you'll have on the operation.

Professional photographers usually go one step further: They choose one camera, one film and developer combination, and stick to it, unless forced to change by circumstances. Because they earn their livings by their cameras, they find that mistakes are costly, and they tend to be very conservative. They're not willing to try every new film and developer that comes out, and certainly won't use one operationally until they've checked it out thoroughly.

This is a good policy to follow, because the stark fact is that you can't rely on manufacturers' advertisements, nor on the write-ups in photography magazines. Often, you'll see an article that touts a new product as being the best thing since the invention of whipped cream. When you use it, you'll often find this was an exaggeration, partly because the writer was trying to produce and interesting article, and partly because he tested it in special circumstances that showed up its features well. Often, he'll "forget" to mention some drawbacks that will be serious for you, and often he'll use unrealistic standards for comparison.

Sources

1. In one instance, the author accompanied police on a narcotics raid in which they went to the wrong house. The detective responsible for surveillance had driven by several times the day before the raid, unable to stop and take notes because of concern over being observed by the suspect. He didn't remember the location of the front door, or if there even was a front door.

The house faced a freeway, and a "fly-by" on this road, using a camera to take a series of photographs would have been one way to avoid the embarrassing results. At least, it would have been possible to read the house numbers from the photograph.

2. *Fundamentals of Physical Surveillance*, Raymond P. Siljander, B.A., Springfield, IL, C.C. Thomas, Publisher, 1977, p. 205.

3. *Ibid.*, p. 205.
4. *Ibid.*, pp. 169-176.
5. *Police Marksman*, September/October 1982, p. 16.

Additional Sources

Applied Surveillance Photography, Raymond P. Siljander, Springfield, IL, C.C. Thomas, Publisher, 1975.

Surveillance and Undercover Investigation, Art Buckwalter, Woburn, MA, Butterworth Publishers, 1983, pp. 117-126.

Kodak Infrared Films, Publication M-18, Eastman Kodak.

Applied Infrared Photography, Publication M-18, Eastman Kodak.

Photographic Surveillance Techniques for Law Enforcement Agencies, Publication M-8, Eastman Kodak.

ELECTRONIC SURVEILLANCE

Possibly the most distorted and romanticized aspect of surveillance is the electronic field. We read of exotic techniques used by secret government agencies, based on "unclassified" releases, but what we don't see are the drawbacks.

Electronic bugs tend to be expensive and unreliable. We see many examples of their use in fiction, and in motion pictures and TV series, but in real life there are some serious problems associated with their use.

One is access to the premises to bug. In many instances, official agents do "black bag jobs" to gain access, but they take a risk when they do this. Without a court order, their careers are hanging out a mile, and can get chopped off summarily if they're caught.

Another is the everyday and annoying problem of battery life. Even with modern electronic technology, battery life is short.[1] Batteries haven't improved much in the last few decades, and we're still far from the point where batteries are as long-lived and reliable as other electronic components.

This means that an agent who places a bug that's battery-operated must return at intervals to change the batteries, which increases his exposure and risk. There are some bugging devices that operate off house current, but their installation is more elaborate, and sometimes requires cutting through a wall to reach the wires. There are other devices that are ready-made to plug-in, bugs disguised as electronic clocks, radios, and lamps, but they have their problems too. Anyone would be suspicious if he came home and found a lamp or radio that he'd never seen before.

Some of the more exotic and spectacular methods written up by popular writers have certain problems, too. An example is the contact, or "spike mike," which the eavesdropper drives into a wall to pick up sounds from the next room. The usual scenario has the agent in a hotel room next to the one occupied by the suspects, listening avidly while they indiscreetly discuss an incriminating subject. While he listens with the earphones, a tape recorder is taking down every word. The reality is quite different. A wall will not only pick up the sound in a room, it will conduct sound. If the room is anywhere near an elevator shaft, the mike will pick up the rumble of the elevator. If there's an air conditioner in the room, the wall will conduct the sound of the mechanism, obliterating any speech picked up from the air.

Another exotic device, supposedly used by the CIA and other arcane government agencies, is the microwave or laser eavesdropper. Supposedly, by beaming this device at a window from a long way off, you can pick up speech in the room. The sound makes the window-glass vibrate, and the laser or microwave beam reflects back to the agent, who has a receiver, amplifier, and tape recorder to capture it all. The unfortunate facts about this method are that a window is mounted in a windowframe, in the wall, and that the window has two sides. Building noises will also make the glass vibrate, as will noise from the street.

If an agent installs a tape recorder on the premises, he has to return periodically to change the tapes. Even with voice-activated recorders (VOX), tape life is short, and it's not possible to get more than about ten hours on a tape. This is why the trend is to install a bug transmitter, which sends a signal that an agent, located nearby, can pick up and tape record right there. Such an arrangement eliminates the need to enter to change tapes. There are problems with this approach, too. Most of these subminiature transmitters have very short ranges, and finding a convenient place nearby to hide while recording their signals can be difficult.

With all that, there are some projects that the civilian can undertake if he needs to "bug" someone, and in many instances he can do so without the risks that government agents take.

Contrary to what some people believe, it's both possible and legal for you to install a bug, in many cases. The chances are you're not looking for evidence that will stand up in court, but merely for information. This allows you more latitude. The chances are, too, that you don't need to gain access to the premises by illegal means, and this clears the way for you, both legally and practically.

For example, someone worried about a spouse's fidelity need not break in to bug his own bedroom. It's very easy to conceal a microphone and VOX tape recorder to monitor the room while away at work. An employer concerned about employee theft has the legal right to install closed-circuit TV in his place of business.

The practicalities have improved, too, during the last few decades. While batteries are still temperamental and unreliable, the equipment is much better. A simple portable radio receiver used to weigh several pounds, and require another several pounds of batteries to operate. The current drain, with tubes, was so heavy that hardly any receiver could operate for more than ten hours from one set of batteries. Today, with solid-state circuitry, it's common to have small, shirt-pocket sized radios that operate for several dozen hours with one nine-volt battery that weighs only a couple of ounces.

Similarly, we find other equipment, such as tape recorders, in which battery life is extended because of low current drain. Microphones, amplifiers, and recording devices don't use much current. There are some devices that do, because of inherent limitations. There are transmitters, electric motors, and loudspeakers. Even here, there are design compromises available which reduce battery drain. Tape recorders, for example, that use cassettes have much smaller motors for tape transport than do the large reel-to-reel types.

The electronic revolution has made available equipment that is low-priced and fairly reliable for the private individual who wants to bug someone else. Formerly, such equipment was available only to those who had large budgets, such as law-enforcement agencies, but today it's within reach of almost anyone. Let's look at specific equipment and techniques.

Telephone Tapping

This is the easiest project, requiring the least equipment. The simplest way to do it is to tap directly into the telephone wires, and connect headphones or an earphone. Figure 8 shows ways to connect the tap. Installation "A" shows headphones connected in parallel. This has the advantage of not lowering the volume in the user's phone, but it also means it's

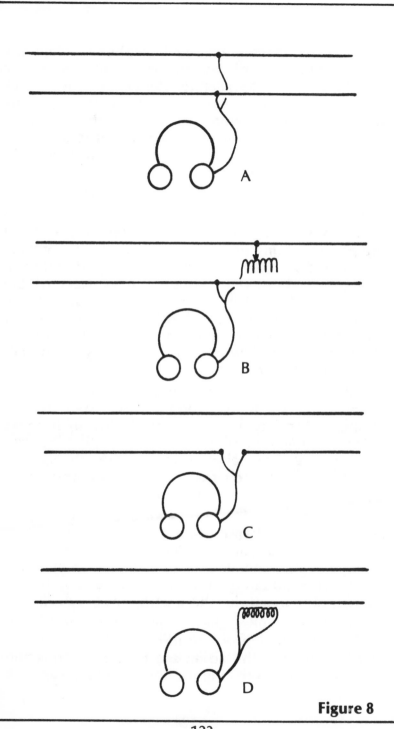

Figure 8

123

necessary to disconnect the headphones when the conversation is finished, to allow the automatic telephone system to hang up. This can produce a click in the line, when connecting or disconnecting. One way to avoid this is set-up "B," putting a rheostat in the line between one connection and the headphone. This allows a slow and gradual connection, and avoids any suspicious sounding clicks.

Another way of using system "B" is to have a capacitor instead of a rheostat in the lines to the headphones. This will not permit current to pass when the phone is hung up, thereby allowing the switching system to disconnect. One problem is that the ringing voltage may burn out the headphones. Keeping the rheostat connected in series with the capacitor will help prevent this. Turning the rheostat to low will cut down the voltage that hits the headphone, low enough to avoid burning them out, yet high enough to permit you to hear the ring.

System "C," a wiring in series, allows a permanent connection, but it may reduce the current to the phone, and this may arouse suspicion. Wiring in series means making your connections and cutting the wire in between. This also increases the chances of detection if anyone checks the line with sophisticated equipment, such as an induction meter.

The last method, "D," uses an induction coil to pick up the telephone transmission. This requires no cutting of the line, no physical connection to it, and is much easier to install and much harder to detect. It works because the pulsating current in the telephone line induces a current in the nearby coil, which the headphones can pick up. It sometimes requires an amplifier to increase the power from the coil.

One conveniently available package is the Radio Shack #42-231, combining the induction pick-up with an amplifier. It costs $9.95, runs off a nine-volt battery, and if you're near the telephone line it will pick up the conversation, amplify it, and play it through a built-in loudspeaker. The problem with it is that you must be listening in another room, and the sound may carry.

Another device, for the person who has convenient access, is the Multi-extension Recording Control, made by Radio Shack to sell for $24.95. This device, catalog number 43-236, plugs right into the wall jack and allows connecting a VOX tape recorder. This allows you to install it and leave the premises. Any telephone conversations will be on the tape when you return. The only problem with this is that you must find a place to conceal it. If there are many phone outlets, and some of them are behind curtains, furniture, or in unused rooms, concealment will be much easier.

If you're even slightly handy at wiring, you can strip off the phone plug of these units and connect them anyplace you have access to the telephone line.

One caution regarding hooking anything up to a telephone line is to do it when the phone is not in use. Any cutting will make clicks in the receiver, and this may alert the person you're trying to bug. An induction coil, however, doesn't pose this problem.

With some skill in electronics, it's possible to combine some off-the-shelf components into custom installations. While having the wire-tapping device on the premises is very helpful and convenient if you have legitimate and regular access, you'll have a problem if you can't gain such access. In such a case, you'll need to have a remote unit. Installing a wiretap hooked up to a transmitter, conventional or CB, will let you pick up and record conversations from outside.

A way to tap into a telephone line at a remote point is to trace the wire visually to a junction box, and make the connections there. The junction box is a piece of telephone company equipment that holds pairs of wires from a number of subscribers, and it may be located in the basement of an apartment or office building, inside a metal box in an alley, or up on a telelphone pole. Connecting to it requires using your eyes and ears, and common sense.

You have to follow the line until you find the convenient junction box. The next step is to find the right pair of wires. This can be done through a direct trace, or by trial and error. If your target is using the phone, tapping pairs until you hear a familiar voice will do. If not, having a friend ring his line steadily while you're searching will disclose the correct line to you. A detailed and somewhat technical discussion of the procedure is publicly available.[2]

Connecting to a junction box has its risks. There's a good chance that a telephone company employee will find your tap. In such a case, you can expect him to disconnect it and report the incident. If your tap is a wired one, and you're at the other end of the wire, you can expect trouble. This is why the best way to do it is with a wireless installation. There's no physical connection between you and the tap, and it's much harder to find you and establish a case for prosecution. This advantage is enough to overcome the other problems connected with taps that operate by radio.

If you have access to the premises, connecting the tap to a VOX tape recorder is one way to do it. You may be able to do this very easily, if your tap has a jack that plugs into the tape recorder, but if not, it's easy to attach a suitable jack. These are readily available for a dollar or two from Radio Shack, and many other electronic outlets.[3]

Bugging

This requires a microphone and wires to connect to headphones or a tape recorder. A small, flat microphone is the Radio Shack #33-1089, for $12.95, made for recording in a room. Hiding this microphone and leading the wires to a remote listening point definitely requires access for a couple of hours. It's necessary to find a hiding place for the microphone, then for the wires. Finding a nearby listening post that you can occupy, or at least visit at intervals, may be difficult.

In placing the microphone, look carefully at the whole room before making your decision. Look for anything that makes noise, keeping in mind that an air conditioner or refrigerator that sounds like a whisper in the room will make a roar into a microphone placed close to it.

Running the wires is usually the biggest problem. You can't leave them out in the open. One way is to run them under a carpet. Another way is to run them behind the molding and through a hole drilled into the wall.

As with telephone taps, the biggest drawback is that there are wires that can lead right to you. If you happen to own the premises, this will be no problem, but if you've entered illegally, you're in trouble.

You can gain partial protection by using a VOX tape recorder, returning regularly to change the tapes and batteries. A tape recorder which has VOX and is cheap and easily available is the Radio Shack CTR-75, for $59.95. A miniature one, pocket-size, is the Radio Shack Micro-15, at $69.95. This reduces your exposure time, but it won't be much help if someone detects your bug, follows the wires, and stakes out the tape recorder. You may choose to gain greater safety by using a wireless system.

Wireless Bugging

This requires a microphone and small transmitter. A microphone small enough to hide can pick up the sound in a room, and feed it into a transmitter that will beam it to you, if you're within range.

Hiding a microphone from casual search is not a serious problem in most rooms. Some possible locations are behind a curtain, fastened to the underside of furniture, and behind furniture. Concealing a bugging device against a skilled and determined search is almost impossible. The main requirement, therefore, is that your target have no suspicion. If you take some care installing the device, he won't become suspicious.

A wireless microphone that transmits up to 250 feet outdoors is the Radio Shack #33-1076, for $19.95. Indoors, you can expect a much shorter range. You can use an ordinary FM receiver to pick up the transmission. One problem with this miciophone-transmitter combination is that it transmits on the FM band, which means that anyone within range can pick up the signal if the radio happens to be tuned to the same frequency. This unit is battery-operated, which makes concealment very easy.

A somewhat larger unit is the Radio Shack #32-1221, which is a two-part unit with its own receiver and a subminiature microphone. This sells for $69.95, and has a range of up to 200 feet. Its main advantage is that it's a high-fidelity unit, which delivers cleaner sound. A serious limitation is that it requires plugging into the household power supply.

The big weaknesses of wireless bugs are the possibility of someone picking up the transmissions accidently, their short ranges, and interference. To some extent, these disadvantages are mutually exclusive. The short ranges of these transmitters cause you a problem, as you have to find a listening post nearby, but they also reduce the chances of accidental pickup.

The short range may mean that you have to operate from your car, parked nearby. In this sense, electronic bugging becomes much like a stake out, and you have to observe the same precautions. You'll probably find that a pick-up truck or camper is more suitable for your purpose than a passenger car, and a motor home best of all.

Interference is hard to predict. There may be a power line nearby, or another source of electromagnetic radiation, which may override your signal. Sometimes it's possible to get rid of interference by changing frequencies, but this requires access to the transmitter. This is why it's a good idea to do a quick test of the equipment right in the area before installing it.

Checking Out Your Equipment

While it's possible today to buy at very low cost what used to be within the budget only of large agencies years ago, some of the equipment is junk. This is why it's important to check out any such material before putting it to use. You'll want to know how well it transmits, how clear the sound reproduction is, how long the range, and its susceptibility to interference. A practical test of battery life may be important, too.

Checking it out has two stages, testing each piece individually, to verify that it works before the warranty runs out, and testing it as part of the system. You'll want to make sure that the combination holds together, and gives you the results you want. When combining components, too, there's always room for error. You simply may not have the pieces wired together right.

With wireless systems, you'll need to adjust the transmitter to operate on the same frequency as your receiver. With the FM types, you'll need to find a spot on the FM band between local stations, so that you'll be able to pick up the transmissions without the stronger commercial signals overriding yours.

Outdoor Eavesdropping

The "Bionic Ear" is a device that uses a directional microphone and an amplifier to pick up sounds at long range. It works off a nine-volt battery, and is a good outdoor eavesdropping device. With it, you can pick up conversations at several hundred yards. It's available mail-order from Parallex Corporation, 1285 Mark St, Bensenville, IL 60106. The toll-free number is 800-323-3233.

There are other models available along the same lines. Hunting, sporting, and survival magazines regularly carry advertisements for similar devices, most of them more expensive.

Protecting Yourself Against Eavesdropping

While you're thinking of doing it to someone, someone may be doing it to you. This section will outline some protective measures, both for your direct use, and to give you an insight into how your target may work to counteract your bugging.

One way to overcome a room bug is to create interference. Holding a conversation in the bathroom or kitchen, with the water running, is a way of creating "white noise" that makes it almost impossible to distinguish speech. Turning on the radio or TV is another way of obscuring a conversation.

There are sophisticated electronic filters that can screen out much of this interfering noise, but they're very expensive and usually only within the reach of government agencies. Most buggers will be stymied by the interference you create.

It used to be that going for a walk outdoors was protection against eavesdropping, but parabolic microphones, directional microphones, and small light-weight amplifiers have now made the outdoors open to eavesdroppers.

The first step in finding a telephone bug is to examine very closely every inch of the phone and its wiring. While some devices pick up without tapping into the wires, they have to be very close to work, and they're too big to hide. Look for a small cylinder or cube an inch or smaller. This is an induction coil.

The search must extend outside your premises, to the junction box, where your wires are connected to the main cable. This will detect unofficial efforts at wiretapping. You should be aware, however, that if a government agency is tapping your line, the agents don't need to connect at the junction box. If they have a court order, or if they have good contacts at the telephone company, they can tap your line right at the central office, and there's no way for you to detect this.

Some precautions against wiretapping are to conduct all sensitive conversations from pay phones, which are unlikely to be tapped. Beware of any near police stations, courts, or government facilities. They may be tapped as a precaution.

Another, more expensive way is to use a scrambler device. These are not commonly available, and are expensive. The simple ones are easy to unscramble, while the more secure digital systems are extremely expensive, virtually priced out of sight.

Searching a room physically gives some protection, at least against the rudimentary bugs. A well-made and well-disguised bug can pass unnoticed in a search, however. There are devices that fit inside wall sockets, have tiny microphones, and transmit over the house wiring. This sort of device is impossible to find without a very detailed search.

For transmitters, there are several ways of countering them. One way is to search for them electronically. Every radio transmitter gives off electromagnetic radiation, and this is easy to locate with a special instrument.

A field-strength meter will pick up radio transmissions, and is a low cost way to tell if you're being bugged. One such is the Radio Shack #21-525, for $18.95, which is small enough to hold in one hand. This allows you to sweep it around the room to pick up suspicious transmissions.

Once you find a bug, what do you do with it? The obvious answer is to deactivate it, but there might be a better' way. If you've been able to find it without creating the sounds of search, the person bugging you might be unaware that his device has been discovered, and you have the prospect of using it to feed him false information.

This is really the best method. If you deactivate the device, your opponent may well plant another. In fact, he might already have done so, leaving one easy to find, in the hope that you'll stop your search once you've found it, and he can continue to eavesdrop with you unaware.

The only safe assumption if you find a bug is that there's another, or perhaps many more. This will put you in the right frame of mind to play a deception operation. With the right tactics, you can lead the eavesdropper on a wild goose chase by feeding him false information.

Advanced Technical Methods

This chapter has been a guide for someone with little or no technical skill. Some people, however, have the education and the eagerness to branch out to use more sophisticated methods. For those interested in more sophisticated applications, there are some books that give the technical background and practical advice to use complex eavesdropping methods:

Methods of Electronic Audio Surveillance, David A. Pollock, Springfield, IL, Charles C. Thomas, Publisher, 1979. This is a book that takes you from A to Z, with a section on basic electrical theory, and the rest devoted to the equipment and its practical applications.

The Big Brother Game, Scott French, Secaucus, NJ, Lyle Stuart, 1976. This is a simplified and popularized book on many aspects of investigation. The section on wiretapping and eavesdropping is a start in understanding this subject, and will serve as background for a more serious study.

How To Avoid Electronic Eavesdropping and Privacy Invasion, William Turner, Boulder, CO, Paladin Press, 1975. This is a nuts-and-bolts manual on how to counteract eavesdropping, whether on the telephone or by more involved bugging techniques. It's a gold mine of information, although poorly organized and relatively hard to read. It doesn't even have an index, but it's worth reading because it's short and sweet.

Sources

1. *Covert Surveillance & Electronic Penetration*, edited by William B. Moran, Port Townsend, WA, Loompanics Unlimited, 1983, p. 11.

2. *Ibid.*, p. 34.

3. Radio Shack is but one source of supply. It's included here because it's a nationwide company with many convenient outlets, but there are other electronic suppliers, including hobby shops, with suitable equipment. The prices quoted here are from the catalog, and some of these items are less costly when they go on sale. Other suppliers make equipment that costs even less, depending on the item and the source.

YOU WILL ALSO WANT TO READ:

Now available:
THE BEST BOOK CATALOG IN THE WORLD!!!

- *Large 8½ x 11 size!*
- *More than 500 of the most controversial and unusual books ever printed!!!*
- *YOU can order EVERY book listed!!!*
- *Periodic Supplements to keep you posted on the LATEST titles available!!!*

We offer hard-to-find books on the world's most unusual subjects. Here are a few of the topics covered IN DEPTH in our exciting new catalog:

- *Hiding/concealment of physical objects! A complete section of the best books ever written on hiding things!*
- *Fake ID/Alternate Identities! The most comprehensive selection of books on this little-known subject ever offered for sale! You have to see it to believe it!*
- *Investigative/Undercover methods and techniques! Professional secrets known only to a few, now revealed for YOU to use! Actual police manuals on shadowing and surveillance!*
- *And much, much more, including Locks and Locksmithing, Self Defense, Intelligence Increase, Life Extension, Money-Making Opportunities, and much, much more!*

Our book catalog is truly THE BEST BOOK CATALOG IN THE WORLD! Order yours today -- you will be very pleased, we know.

(Our catalog is free with the order of any book on the previous page -- or is $2.00 if ordered by itself.)